Mercedes

Mercedes

Nigel Fryatt

MALLARD
PRESS

Page 1: Mercedes-Benz means a certain style. The familiar shape of the SL roadster, this time the 230 SL, high in the Austrian Tirol.

Page 2 and 3: The power package. These three fabulous versions of the 190 saloon represent the development of the road-going version necessary for the marque to participate in European saloon car racing.

This page: The 1914 Mercedes Grand Prix racing car was way ahead of its time. Its four cylinder, four valve per cylinder, single overhead camshaft engine produced 115bhp and was capable of 112mph. It was also capable of a one-two-three victory at the 1914 French GP – the last GP before the outbreak of World War One.

Contents

Creating a Great Name

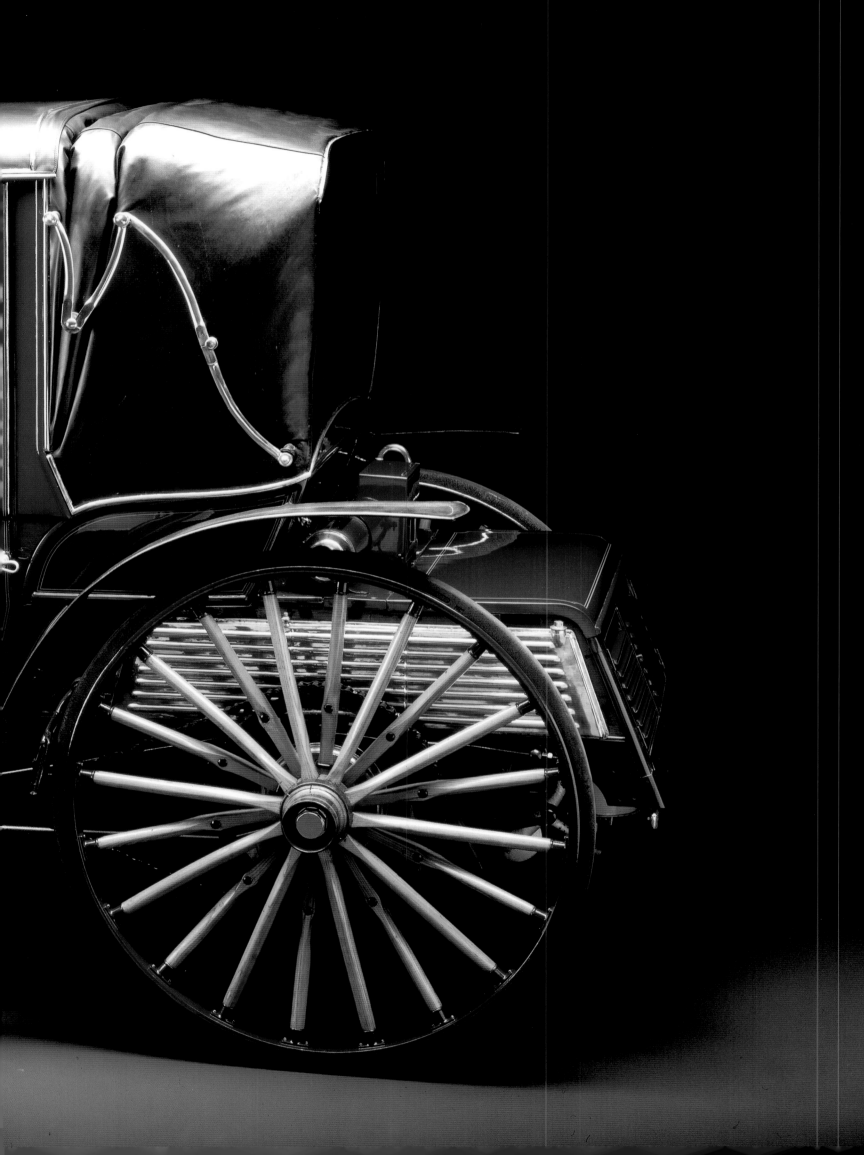

And to think, they never met. Two of the founding fathers of the modern automobile, Gottlieb Daimler and Karl Benz, began their work a mere 60 miles apart, yet surprisingly never actually worked together. When the two companies finally amalgamated in 1926, Benz was in his eighties and Daimler had died a quarter of a century before. That this company exists today is a credit to the men, that the company produces some of the most desirable luxury cars in the world is a testament to the foundations laid by the two pioneers and the strength and quality of the product that followed. Their names are synonymous with prestige automobiles – but where does Mercedes come in? Just wait a while, that would be jumping ahead a few years.

First we need to go back to 1886, the year that both Daimler and Benz produced gasoline driven vehicles. But before we do, consider first that it is difficult to argue just who invented the first 'car' – as we understand the definition today. There were steam powered monsters a century before Daimler and Benz and certainly by the late 1800s, there were others who produced 'horseless carriages'. However, it is easy to say that Daimler and Benz stand ahead of the inventors of these other contraptions because they succeeded in progressing the design, refining it, turning it into what you and I would recognise as a car.

Gottlieb Daimler was ten years older than Benz and so it makes sense to look at his early work first. A talented student, Daimler worked for a gunmaker, in a locomotive works, but it was not steam that interested the young engineer. He travelled to England where he worked for two British engineering companies before returning to Germany and working for Otto and Langen, makers of the four-stroke natural gas engine. It was here that Daimler's single-mindedness was evident. He wanted to progress the design, and do more research while his employers – perhaps understandably - wanted him to work in the production of the current products. Daimler, therefore, decided to leave and spent a brief period working in Russia for an oil company before he decided to set up his own engineering company.

Previous page: The quality of workmanship on the 1899 Benz is apparent from this picture. The 2.7-liter two cylinder engine was capable of nearly 25mph.

Left: This 1899 wire wheeled Daimler was a significant move away from the horseless carriage concept. The first development of which had been seen in 1886. This model (*below left*) used the single cylinder engine designed and built by Gottlieb Daimler (*below*) and his partner Wilhelm Maybach (*below right*). The apparent simplicity of these early Daimlers (*right*) should not be allowed to cloud the fact that they represented highly significant breakthroughs in the history of the automobile.

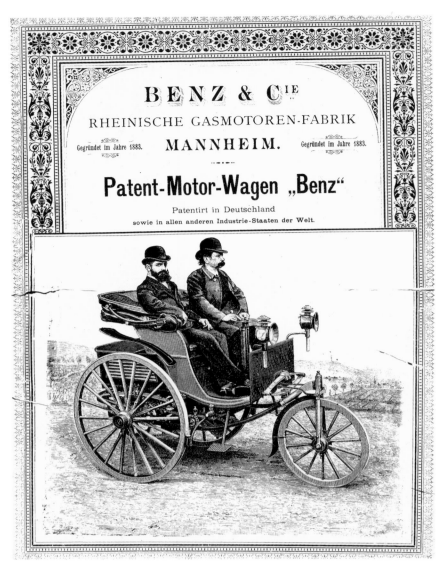

BENZ & CIE

RHEINISCHE GASMOTOREN-FABRIK

MANNHEIM.

Gegründet im Jahre 1883.   Gegründet im Jahre 1883.

Patent-Motor-Wagen „Benz"

Patentirt in Deutschland
sowie in allen anderen Industrie-Staaten der Welt.

Not everyone at Otto and Langen was against Daimler, chief designer Wilhelm Maybach shared his dream and joined the new company set up in Bad Cannstatt in 1882. As in all the best stories, the first location was far from ideal, in this case a converted summerhouse, but they soon moved to a small factory.

A mere 12 months after the inauguration of the new company, Daimler took out a patent on his first engine. This single cylinder unit was unique in that it did not run on natural gas. Daimler and Maybach had managed to develop an ignition system which would allow the unit to run on benzine or gasoline. It is important to realise here that you must not take for granted that everyone was working towards a gasoline-powered engine. They were not. Gasoline was only available from pharmacists at the time. Daimler's engine would also run at speeds up to 900rpm – unheard of at the time.

But Daimler's vision was far wider than just developing the automobile. In 1885 he built a motorcycle, powered by an air-cooled engine developing 0.5bhp. There was even a marine section to the Daimler company, and this was set to flourish when the Prince Bismarck gave his blessing to one design and bought one of the boats.

One must not get the opinion that in Germany at this time, all the engineering developments were the work of this one man. There was also the younger Karl Benz. Like Daimler he proved a talented student and graduated from the Karlsruhe Polytechnic, worked for a short while as a locksmith and then as a fitter at a locomotive works. Just like Daimler, this period made him realise the limited future of steam as a means of propulsion. Benz, however, was more convinced of the possibilities of gas. This was already being piped throughout towns and seemed therefore to be a suitable source of energy. Benz and Company was set up in Mannheim in 1886 to produce gas-engines.

If it seems that Benz was a little behind Daimler in using natural gas instead of gasoline, that would be wrong. Looking at the works of the two men – occurring independently don't forget – where one was slightly ahead in one department, he was behind in another. Benz, for instance, had the edge in the ignition side having electronic ignition as early as 1886. It was this year that he produced his first three wheeler. The first 'real car'? As we have said

earlier, this is an argument that will run and run, but despite only being a three wheeler (Benz at the time had not managed to solve the steering problems of four wheeled designs) it had a list of technical characteristics that are still with us today. Besides electronic ignition, the single cylinder engine was water-cooled, had mechanically operated inlet valves, and a very clever differential. It was regularly seen around the streets of Mannheim and was capable of 7.5mph (12kmph). This was quite a startling sight and not one that was well received by public and police. Despite being awarded the prestigious Gold Medal at the 1888 Munich Exhibition, pressure from the authorities was against the machine, this deterred sales and saw the company struggle. Benz's financial supporters grew impatient and withdrew, putting the whole project in jeopardy.

The authorities even made a rule that the three-wheeler could not be taken outside the town limits of Mannheim. This was a restriction that did not please one of the pioneer 'drivers' of the period, Benz's wife Bertha. The story goes that one morning she took one of the three-wheelers without her husband's knowledge (was this the first recorded auto theft?) and went to see her mother in Pforzheim. The 112 mile round trip is now the stuff of motoring legend. The story is embellished with reports of incidents on the trip including having to use her hat pin to clear a fuel blockage, a piece of garter elastic to repair a broken spring in the ignition system and a visit to a cobbler to provide some new leather padding for the brakes. Quite a story, and whether it is all true is, in my opinion, irrelevant.

One man who also believed in Benz was Julius Ganss, a very clever and persuasive salesman. It was Ganss, rather than the resourceful Bertha Benz, who managed to find markets for the three-wheeler that kept the project moving. Benz and Company were also involved in producing stationary engines and this side of the business flourished during this period, which allowed Benz himself to concentrate on his automobiles. The problem with the steering was overcome and his assistant August Horch managed to produce more power from the engines. In 1894, Benz produced the Velo, claimed to be the first car in the world to be built in series production. Its 1050cc, single cylinder engine produced 1.5bhp.

Left: Is this the first automobile? That argument will run and run, but the 1886 Benz three wheeler will always have a strong claim. Benz had yet failed to solve the problems of steering two front wheels. Despite advertising the machine (*above left*) and being acclaimed by the press the three wheel design was restricted by the Mannheim authorities. In Stuttgart, Gottlieb Daimler was promoting his four wheeled designs (*above*). Early Benz four wheelers, like the 1891 Vis-a-vis (*below*), were large cumbersome looking devices.

Left: The 1894 Benz Velo was the world's first series motor car. It was also entered into the first recorded motor race, the Paris – Rouen, held the same year.

Right: The Velo was powered by a single cylinder engine of 1050cc capacity producing 1.5hp.

Below: Karl Benz was the son of a railway mechanic and his father died when he was very young. His upbringing was obviously very difficult, but his mother ensured that he gained a good education; an education that soon inspired his love of things mechanical.

It was at this period that the two companies actually met – in the heat of competition. The Velo was entered in the Paris-Rouen race. It is said that Benz was against motorsport but could obviously see its possibilities in establishing his designs. His antipathy could well have been fuelled, however, by the fact that most of this sport occurred in France and his cars were entered by his French importer Emile Roger. The success of the Frenchman led to many referring to the cars as 'Rogers'. The French were the speed crazy nation and all motorsport owes its origins to this country's enthusiasm.

It was at this time that Daimler's cars 'changed name' too. By 1900 Daimler was actually a very sick man, but he was still working on improving his designs and at this time incorporated the work of Robert Bosch significantly to improve the ignition system. He also began to use the new pneumatic tires and produced a new 6hp four-cylinder machine after an enquiry from Austrian businessman Emile Jellinek.

This car was the Phaeton, was capable of 26mph (42kmph) and handled very well. It was not, however, quick enough to beat the French. The more powerful Daimler Phoenix followed, built purely to race and this car led to the death of the works driver Wilhelm Bauer on the La Turbie hill climb. The accident led to Daimler withdrawing from competition but Emile Jellinek did not agree with that. A banker, businessman and diplomat, Jellinek also distributed Daimlers and was a firm enthusiast of the marque. He demanded that the factory build a longer wheelbase machine, with a lower center of gravity and an even more powerful engine. To help persuade Daimler he agreed to buy 36 of these cars (before they had been built remember) if he could have the distribution rights for Austria, France, Belgium, Hungary and – with great foresight – America and provided, and here's the important part, he could call the cars after his daughter, Mercedes.

Jellinek had previously used the name Mercedes when racing, a not uncommon action used by the gentry to prevent social disapproval. Although the name is actually of Spanish origin, it sounded French, aided by the fact that to start with the name carried the two accents, later to be dropped. Whether Daimler approved of the scheme is uncertain, as it was obvious to all around him that he was close to death, but it was agreed with Maybach and fellow directors and so the deal was made. The whim of an Austrian motorsporting enthusiast to use his daughter's name has now become one of the most famous and recognised automobile marques in the entire world.

was capable of 53mph (85kmph). In March 1901 it completely dominated the Nice Speed Week. It looked different to everything else and it performed better. There were others with larger engines, but Maybach had already realised that a balance had to be struck between engine power and handling and with some new chassis pressings had produced a car that drove better than its competitors. And so, with the turn of the century, Mercedes cars were leading the field.

But things were changing very rapidly in the burgeoning automotive field. 1900 also began with the death of Gottlieb Daimler at the age of 66. The company was in the hands of his two sons Adolf and Paul and financier Max Duttenhofer, but all the important work was being done by engineer Maybach.

The Mercedes 35hp which had caused such a sensation only two years before was humiliated in the prestigious Paris-Berlin race of 1902, managing only 14th place. Defeat stimulated Maybach to design a car to meet the new 'lighter' motorsporting formula. These 40hp racers were known as Mercedes-Simplex and they were matched with a complete model range; the 12/16, 18/22, 28/32 and 40/45. If these model titles seem rather odd, they actually make a lot of sense; the first number is the taxable horsepower of the car and the second its effective output. Racing cars were not taxed and so were only known by the single set of figures denoting the power.

1903 was an action-packed 12 months for the Daimler factory. They entered the Paris-Madrid race, joining over 100 similar cars. Remember that these races were on public roads — little more than tracks in most places of course — and safety was a very low priority. Racing had become very important, however, and there were cars from Germany, France, Italy and Britain. A series of terrible accidents in which spectators as well as competitors were killed saw the French authorities stop the race at Bordeaux. It was the last of the epic city-to-city marathons.

But it was not the end of motorsport. The Gordon Bennett Trophy had been instigated by American James Gordon Bennett, owner of the *New York Times*, to raise the profile of international motor racing especially in the United States. The rules stated that the race would be run in the country of the previous year's winner. In 1902, a Napier driven by S. F. Edge had won which meant the 1903 event should be held in Britain. However, the appalling accidents in France led to a government ban in England so the race moved to Ireland. Daimler had built no less than five cars for the Trophy but

The first Mercedes was a stunning sensation. Maybach took Jellinek's idea and produced a highly innovative machine. For the first time on any car, it had a honeycomb radiator, a foot throttle, an integral crankcase and four-speed transmission with column-mounted gear shift. The 5.9-liter engine with its mechanically operated valves and Bosch low-tension magneto ignition which could be manually retarded or advanced, produced 35bhp and

Left: Even as early as the turn of the twentieth century, the value of publicity photographs was obvious to both Benz and Daimler. The *top* picture has the Benz family enjoying an afternoon's drive — the two girls in front being his daughters Clara and Tilde. The *bottom* photograph shows an 1899 Daimler Taxi which — if we are to believe the expression of the male passenger — was the only way for the gentry to travel.

Above: The face that launched many million cars! This is Mercedes, the daughter of the Austrian businessman, Emile Jellinek. It was he who began importing Daimlers throughout Europe and America providing he could call the cars after his daughter. How lucky we are she had such an evocative name . . .

Right: The Benz Dos-a-Dos was one of the first of his cars to use the horizontally opposed twin-cylinder engine. This unit produced some 4.5hp.

these were all destroyed in a major fire at the factory. Nevertheless, the Belgian tire maker Camille Jenatzy borrowed a 60hp Mercedes and won against very strong opposition. It was a major triumph for the German manufacturer.

It was also the last major success for Daimler during this period. The French went on to dominate motor sport for the next few years; Wilhelm Maybach left to set up his own company making engines for cars and later for the Zeppelin airships; and Emile Jellinek, the highly influential world wide distributor retired through ill-health. Sales dropped and Daimler cut its work force by almost 50 percent in the years 1907-8.

There had been lean years for Karl Benz too. He was never a great believer in motorsport and had stuck with his original designs. In the early years they were successful, but as others became more advanced, sales dropped. Internal disputes even saw Benz resign from his own company for a time, to return and redevelop a number of older designs. As with Daimler, Benz had been producing cars of modest size and power while also having the quality luxury motor car. In 1905, Benz even put together a list of all the important and titled people who owned one his cars.

The Benz company's first major motorsporting success was, ironically, at a time when Daimler was at its lowest ebb. A 120bhp Benz won a race from St Petersburg to Moscow. The car was designed by Hans Nibel and it was he who did for Benz what Maybach had done for Daimler, heading the company's design team for the next 20 years.

It was Nibel who designed the legendary Blitzen Benz, the racing car winning numerous events and actually holding the land speed record of 141.7mph (228kmph) set in 1909. This surprisingly nimble machine had a series of massive engines rising to no less than 21.5 liters in its largest form and this was only a four cylinder!

1909 was also significant for Daimler as it was the first year that they used the three-pointed star as the company emblem. According to legend, Gottlieb Daimler used to tell his children that a star would rise to bring happiness and good fortune to the family. The Daimler board liked the story and decided to register it as an emblem. At first they registered both three and four-pointed designs but, as we all know, it was the former that has remained with the marque ever since.

These were the years of great strain throughout Europe. Both Daimler and Benz developed their cars, and the Mercedes name returned to motorsport. The 1914 French Grand Prix was, therefore, far more than just a race. Mercedes cars were entered bringing with them a professionalism that had not been seen before, but matches the way the company races today. Metic-

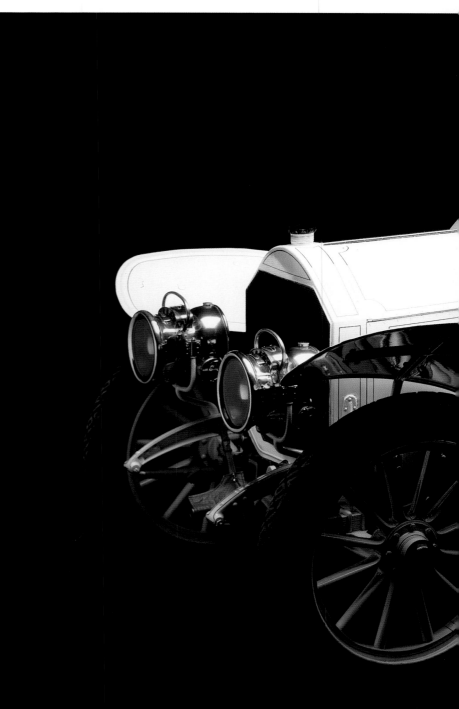

It is important to realise that in the early days, both Benz and Daimler had to rely on producing commercial vehicles. The truck (*left*) and omnibus (*right*) were both examples of 1905 Daimler products.

Below: As early as 1905, Mercedes motor cars were beginning to be built on a grand scale. This is a two seater version of the Simplex range. This highly sporting model had a huge 10-liter power unit and was used by the company in competition. Four seater, family versions were also produced.

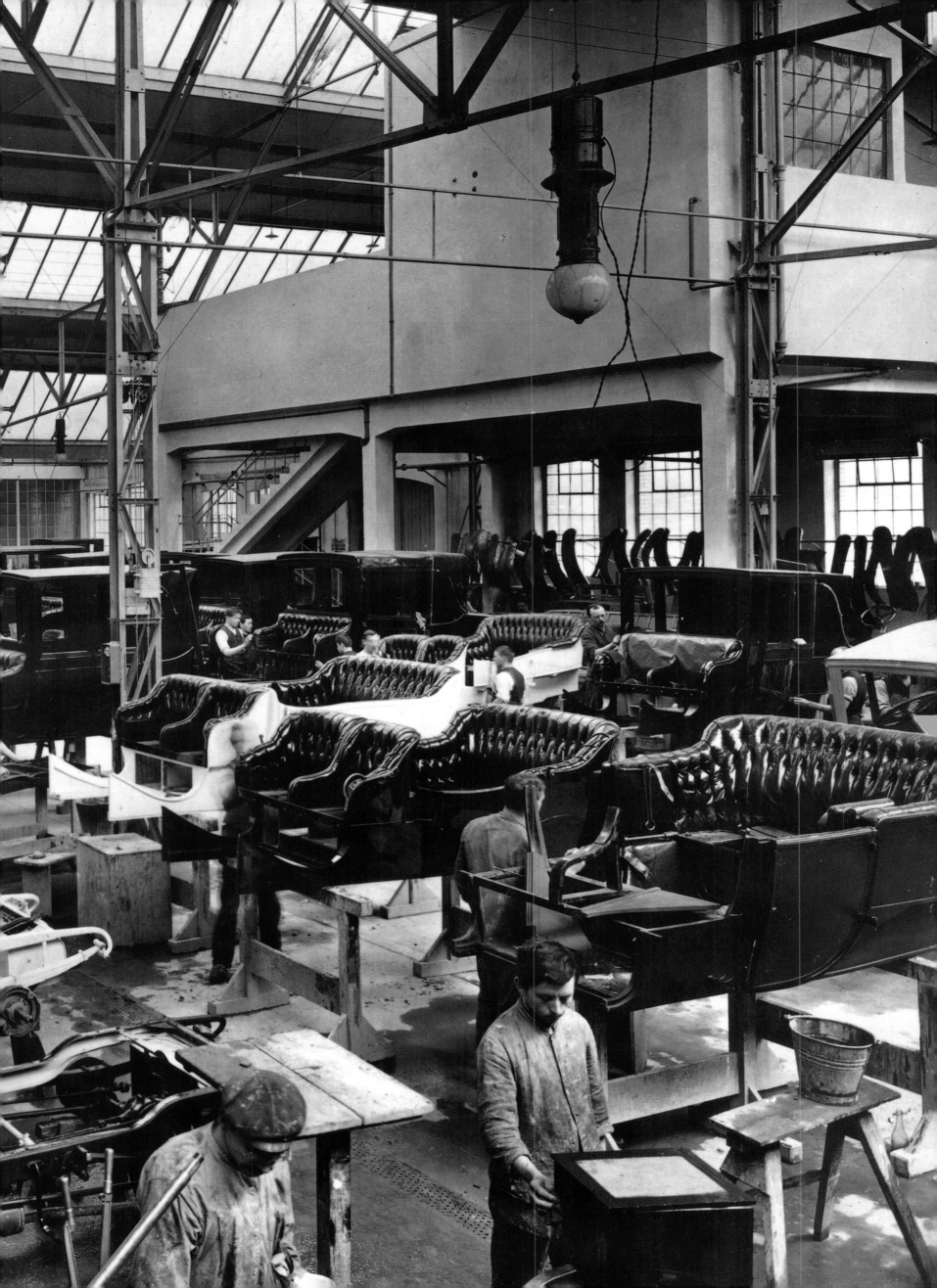

ulous preparation had meant that the entire team had practised at the course for many weeks before the event, the just reward being the first three places. The German victory stunned France. Only months later the two countries were at war.

During the war, both Daimler and Benz turned their factories over to military production both for vehicles and aero-engines. When the conflict was over, Germany was in complete financial ruin. The last thing it needed was a massive motor industry yet, unbelievably, there were no less than 86 different manufacturers throughout the country producing well over 100 different vehicles. With massive inflation and few materials, many companies looked at cheaper products to survive, but both Daimler and Benz now had a world-wide reputation for engineering quality and luxury motor cars and a complete change of direction did not make good sense even in such difficult times.

The German government actually lowered the tax on luxury vehicles but this alone could not guarantee survival, let alone success. The idea of a joint agreement between the two companies was suggested in 1919 but strongly resented by many members of both boards of directors. Pressure mounted, however, and an 'agreement of mutual interest' was signed in 1924 with the two companies merging as Daimler-Benz AG in July 1926.

To signify the merger, the three-pointed star of Mercedes was joined with the laurel leaf used by Benz.

Joint effort from Mercedes-Benz

After the merger, the newly formed company set along a period of consolidation. That's another way of saying that they produced some rather dull, uninspiring motor cars. For the next five years, these bland, conventional vehicles at least added a secure base for the company. The new company produced models with the names Mannheim and Stuttgart to help consolidate the merger in the face of public opinion.

It was not all dull as dishwater, however, since the sedans that were the company's stable diet did allow for some more exciting models to be produced in limited numbers. These were the supercharged sports cars. Starting with the 1926 K (the k was for *kurz*; short) with its 6.25-liter, 160bhp

engine it was one of the most desirable super sports cars of the day – it was also one of the most expensive, but it started a line of superb machinery through the SS to the SSK. These sports cars are detailed further in Chapter Three.

The performance of these cars did, of course lead to their use in motorsport. Men like Caracciola took them to Grands Prix and hillclimb victories across Europe. The 1930s were epic years for the three-pointed star in motorsport (see Chapter Four).

The company's road car program was not left completely behind and was to receive a major boost in 1931 with the 170 series. Chief engineer Hans Nibel was primarily a chassis engineer rather than engine designer. It is no surprise, therefore, that the significance of the 170 was its all-independently sprung lightweight chassis. The 170 was aimed at the medium-sized sector of the market and with this new chassis, had a ride and handling package far ahead of its rivals. It was a package that was represented in the price too. At £375 in Britain in 1931 it put the three-pointed star into a completely new market. This was a very significant mass production model in the Mercedes-Benz story.

In 1936 a diesel engined vehicle was added to top the line-up. The engine had been available in 1922 but the debut of 260D at the Berlin Motor Show gave the company an extremely durable design and the forerunner of a range of cars that are still successful in Europe today.

Towards the end of the 1930s then, Mercedes-Benz had an excellent model range; from diesels to comfortable middle market sedans to luxury supercharged sports cars. Progress was halted, of course, with the Second World War.

The conflict destroyed some 80 percent of the Mercedes-Benz factories and most of the workforce had gone. Technically, immediately after the war, Mercedes-Benz actually ceased to exist. But many of the work force came back. Business began with repair and maintenance jobs while the company planned just how it could start the monumental task of rebuilding and re-manufacture.

Actual manufacturing started again with the 170 and 230 six cylinder sedans. For 1949 an extensively revised 170S was launched. It had actually been run as a prototype before the outbreak of war and it was this model that

Previous page: The Benz production line at Mannheim in 1910. It is clear from this picture how the chassis were built up before the different variety of bodies could be fitted. You can see both open and closed versions being prepared.

Left: This 1922 Mercedes 25hp shows clearly the three-pointed star that was used both on the cars and in the company's poster advertising (*above*).

Right: The 1911 90hp Mercedes, showing the then familiar pointed front radiator.

MERCEDES

Fabrikat der
Daimler-Motoren-Gesellschaft
Stuttgart-Untertürkheim
**Verkaufstellen und Vertretungen in allen
Hauptplätzen des In- und Auslandes**

Mercedes-Benz Publikation um 1920

Sieh die Welt aus Deinem
Mercedes-Benz!

MERCEDES - BENZ
Der Wagen der Extraklasse

firmly re-established the company throughout Europe. The workforce increased, production rose, reputation grew.

The technical foresight of Hans Nibel was also continued. Although the talented engineer had died in 1934, his chassis designs continued for much of the early reconstruction period with the new developments now in the hands of Fritz Nallinger and Rudolf Uhlenhaut. The latter was something of an ace behind the wheel, the story goes that at times he was often quicker when test driving the race cars than the racing drivers the company was employing . . . much to the annoyance of his superiors. He was put in charge of the racing program and was obviously highly influential in the design and development of the 300 range of sports cars of the early 1950s; a range that included one of the best-known and most-easily recognised cars in the history of the automobile – the 1955 300SL 'Gullwing' (see Chapter Three).

The early 1950s were another glorious period in motorsport for the company, soured by the horrendous accident at Le Mans in 1955. The company's total domination of the sport at the time coupled with the bad publicity from the accident – through no fault of Mercedes – prompted a retirement from mainstream motorsport that was not to be reversed until the 1980s (fully detailed in Chapter Four).

From the late 1950s to this present day, the Mercedes range has developed and progressed with safety an underlying factor in design and construction. Safety had always been of great import to the company. Measures in the 180 range meant that as early as 1951 developments were made that prevented the doors of any car remaining locked in the event of an accident. But from 1959 when the original design studies were made for the 220 sedan range, safety was even higher up the list. Some 80 models were crash tested. Extra padding was included in the design to reduce passenger injury. In 1961 the 220SE coupe was the first Mercedes-Benz to be fitted with disc brakes – standard on all models ever since.

Through the sixties, Mercedes-Benz, along with the majority of the other major manufacturers went through a rather dull period with regards to styling. The Mercedes-Benz sedans were conservative and while many of the sports car versions of the period indicated that all was not lost in the visual inspiration department, this is not the most attractive period of the company's history. Even the launch in 1963 of the Pullman Mercedes was not a visual surprise.

Two Pullman models were launched, the 5/6 seater and the 7/8 seater. The 600 models not only had railway carriage seating arrangements but also looked rather like rolling stock in appearance. Performance, however, was another matter. The new 6.3-liter engine had enough power to pull the monsters along at a fine pace. The car was actually bigger than the Rolls-Royce Phantom V and probably had more prestige. The V8 was later to find itself shoe-horned into the shell of a 300, considerably lighter than the Pullman, so the performance was electric.

1972 saw a major development within the company with the launch of the new S-class. These new models were the result of much extensive development using the imaginative C111 experimental coupe (see Chapter Five). The body had its own 'safety cell' welded to a floorpan chassis. Strong, and with all new running gear, it was a great success. In fact, the 450 series (the version fitted with the 4.5-liter V8) was voted Car Of The Year in 1972.

By 1974, Mercedes-Benz led the world in diesel car manufacture and this was set to continue with the recognition that just because someone might opt for a diesel version, they too wanted all the luxury appointments that were now synonymous with the marque. This was further emphasized with the first Middle East fuel crisis of the 1970s where economy was called for but not at the expense of comfort.

One of the most important points to recognise with the success of Mercedes-Benz has been the company's ability subtly to alter the specification of a particular model to meet the niche in the market. Engine permutations across the range have increased over the years and that, coupled with the German public's desire to have badge-less versions of the car, means it can sometimes be very difficult to tell exactly what model you are looking at.

Left: The 1930s and 40s were sombre years for automotive design as can be seen from this six cylinder Type 230.

Above: This model is one of the first produced after the amalgamation – the 1928 Type 260 Mercedes-Benz. Its six cylinder, 2500cc engine produced 50bhp.

Right: This 1947 Type 170 has been converted to run on liquid petroleum gas (not gasoline). Just what would happen in either a front or rear collision does not bear thinking about.

The second important factor in the success has to be the amount of money that is pumped back in through research and development, a lack of which has seen a great number of other manufacturers flounder over that last couple of decades.

In 1979, Mercedes developed in conjuction with Steyr-Daimler-Puch the Gelandewagen range of four-wheel drive off-road vehicles. These are built in Graz, Austria and their military appearances should not disguise the fact that the complete range includes very well-appointed versions and their off-road abilities to plough through the difficult stuff are second only to Land Rover and Range Rover. The interesting technical design of these vehicles is the ability the driver has to lock manually one or both of the differentials in the axles, in the belief that in doing so, should only one wheel be in contact with the ground and have grip, progress may still be possible. It's not quite as simple as that, but it is an interesting technical feature.

With the growing criticism of large luxury cars and their effects on the environment, pressure that is extremely great in Germany, it was no real surprise in 1982 when the new 'small' Mercedes was launched. The W123 model range is known as the 190 and is best described as medium sized, rather than small. Visually in keeping with larger Mercedes, the 190 has been a great sales success and extended the three-pointed star into a much wider market place – a marketing ploy that the company has used previously, of course. The model has done much to increase the financial security to the company and allow it to continue to build exotic, highly desirable sports cars like the latest 500SL announced in early 1989. There will be a new S-class available by the time this book is published with attention to detail in the creature comforts of a motor car almost overwhelming.

Motor sport, too, has seen Mercedes return to the front, winning again at Le Mans with the glorious sports prototype racing Group C Silver Arrow machines.

Undoubtedly the company is stronger than ever before; still producing quality luxury sedans, fast, exotic and desirable sports cars and winning in the even more competitive field of motorsport. A lot has changed in the last 100 years, yet somehow when you look at Mercedes-Benz you feel the two men had it all planned that way, way back in 1886.

Can we really believe they never met?

Above: You have to look twice at this picture not to think it is a Rolls-Royce. Certainly the design of this 1957 300 was aimed directly at the British specialist car maker. The quality and luxury of the model are evident from this picture.

Left: Modern Mercedes-Benz designs have a clean, uncluttered look about them. This is the 560SEC – coupe versions have remained a major part of the Mercedes-Benz range.

Right: The gorgeous 500SL sports car was announced in 1989 and looks like being in demand for many years yet.

The Classic Cars

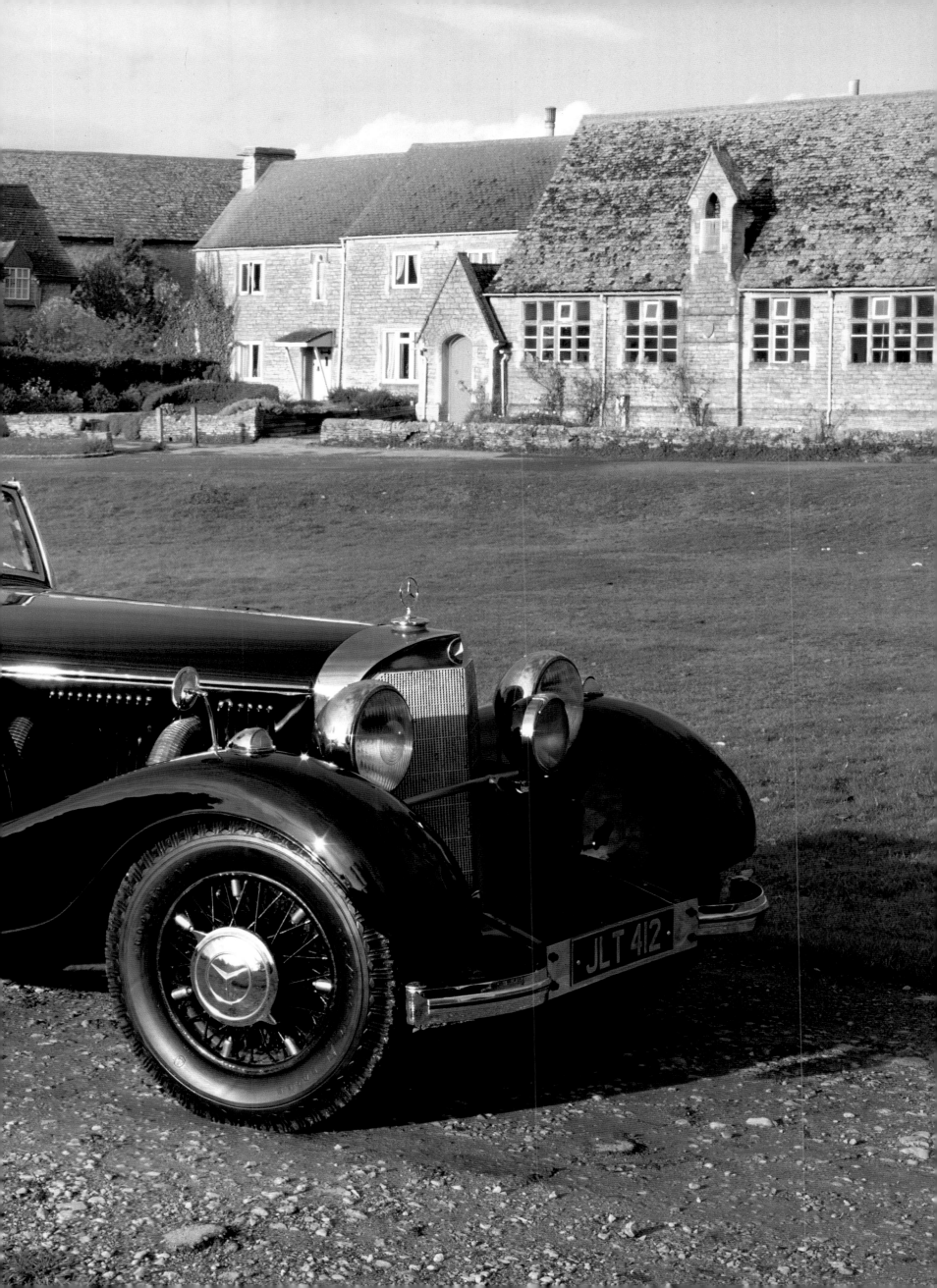

Vehicles bearing the three-pointed star are now renowned for build quality, competence of design and technical excellence. The best way to see how this has been established is to look over the years highlighting the significant models that have built that reputation. From the early models of 1926, to the glorious S-class range of the 1990s the strength of character of the manufacturer is always evident. Put quite simply, Mercedes-Benz has built some excellent automobiles.

Mannheim and Stuttgart

Joining forces

After the co-operation agreement was turning into a full merger, the new company obviously had to rationalise its range, a range which spread across a number of geographically separated manufacturing centers. The results were the Mannheim, Stuttgart and Nürburg sedans each featuring the U-chassics and semi-elliptic leaf springs. This design offered great rigidity which aided the car's handling characteristics, but they were really rather conventional vehicles with rather dull styling. The six cylinder side-valve engines were available in two sizes, 2-liter Stuttgart and 3.1-liter Mannheim. Each had a seven main bearing crankshaft which meant the engines ran very smoothly and were very reliable but with rather plodding performance; the Stuttgart had a top speed of 47mph.

More powerful engines were developed, the 2-liter went up to 2.6 and the 3.1-liter up to 3.5 which helped keep pace with competitors. A larger 4.4-liter eight cylinder model was introduced in 1928 known as the Nürburg. In 1931

this model was capable of producing 110bhp and called the Nürburg 500 and was designed to be a major challenge to the Packard Straight Eight but was not a great success and did not sell well outside Germany. These models can, however, be seen as important for Mercedes-Benz for their ability to create a sturdy sales base for the newly joined company to build upon.

Previous page: This Mercedes-Benz 500K is a rare 1934 version built in right hand drive form and still used in England today.

When the two companies amalgamated, production facilities were spread across Germany. This meant that early models were given the names of the towns in which they were built. This gave us the Nürburg (*above left*) seen here in its Pullman limousine version; the Stuttgart sedan (*left*) and Cabriolet version (*above*) and the Mannheim (*right*).

Grosser

By Royal Command

These models were aimed directly at one particular market; royalty. Extremely luxurious and built in limited numbers, Grosser was big, opulent and extremely well equipped. Kaiser Wilhelm II had one and it is said that the Emperor of Japan actually ordered seven with a couple of the cars remaining in use until very recently.

Constructed on the very sturdy box section chassis frame they were powered by a 7.7-liter straight eight producing 150bhp or up to 200bhp with the addition of the supercharger.

Obviously, as they were built in such small numbers for special clients, the exact specification varied from client to client but one of the most popular versions was the cabriolet.

In 1938 the 770K model was introduced with an uprated chassis of a cruciform backbone frame with swing axle suspension. The same engine was used but uprated slightly to offer more power and making the car capable of just over 100mph; impressive for such a large and heavy machine. The car gained something of an unenviable reputation as being 'staff cars' for the leading members of the Nazi Party. Adolf Hitler often used one on public occasions and for personal and Nazi Party travel around Germany. Plans were in hand to develop the massive sedan further by fitting a version of the V12 engine then used in the Grand Prix cars, but these were shelved with the outbreak of the Second World War.

These were very impressive big sedans with a world-wide reputation now, thanks to many appearances in Hollywood war films and TV specials.

170 and 200

Strength In Numbers

The 170 range marks an important stage in the evolution of the Mercedes-Benz marque. The 1930s were not a great time for building cars, the Depression having knocked the bottom out of the market for luxury cars. There was still a demand for models like the Grosser but that was limited. Mercedes-Benz needed a volume vehicle, a family car.

The 170 was Hans Nibel's first significant mass production design and it gained much from the knowledge that the company had learned from years of motorsport involvement. The 170's lightweight chassis (from the design used in racing) and swing axle combination set standards for ride and handling in the medium sized automobile sector. The chassis was a pressed-steel box section that arched over the rear axle to allow for ample movement of the independent rear suspension. Twin coil springs on each side helped to give the model such good ride quality.

Only modest performance was available from the 1692cc six cylinder side valve engine, which is hardly surprising considering it only produced 32bhp.

Above: The Grosser Mercedes-Benz model was the flagship of the company throughout the 1930s. No expense was spared and the cars were built for the top people, especially popular with Royalty. They have, however, also gained an unenviable reputation from being used by the leading members of the Nazi party (*right*). The top Grosser models weighed some 6000 pounds and were powered by huge 7.7-liter eight cylinder engines. The owner often had a series of buttons – faster, slower, stop, return home – with which he could transfer his commands to his chauffeur without the need to lower himself to verbal instruction.

Above right: Far removed from the luxury of the Grosser models, but far more important for the future of the company, the 1930s saw the introduction of the smaller, 'family', Mercedes-Benz, the Type 170.

The pictures on this spread show the models that became the foundations upon which Mercedes-Benz built its future. Some 14,000 170 models were sold between 1930 and 1935. Despite being relatively inexpensive and mass produced they all had excellent ride quality due to the lightweight chassis and independent suspension for all four wheels. The 170 range had both hard top sedans and cabriolet versions as well as commercial models.

But it was never aimed to be a performance vehicle. A very competitive pricing structure brought the three-pointed star within reach of a much wider market than ever before and no less than 14,000 were built in the first five years.

From 1932, the power was increased with the introduction of the 200s. Similar in design (and now including a cabriolet version) the 200 had a 40bhp version of the six cylinder engine. This model was an even greater success and outsold the 170.

The production lines for the 170 and 200 rather surprisingly survived the ravages of the Second World War. When the hostilities had ceased, all equipment and parts stocks were moved to Unterturkheim. Mercedes-Benz was given permission to start production again and to set up repair and maintenance work. Private cars were not in great demand immediately after the war which is why the first post-war versions of the 170 were commercials — ambulances, pick-ups and delivery vans. In 1949 the 170D was launched, its diesel engine having a similar power output of 38bhp but being important as the economy model of the Mercedes-Benz range.

The significance of the 170 range is that it was the basis for the company's reconstruction, without it, the immediate post-war period could possibly have seen the complete collapse of Mercedes-Benz.

Left: By the mid-1930s, Mercedes-Benz was appealing to a larger audience – many of whom wanted a practical, usable car. Designs, like the 200 shown, became less enterprising, more straightforward.

Below left: The 220 was a development of the 170 and 200 range. This is a 1951 cabriolet version the 220A.

Right: The 1950s saw the introduction of chrome trimmings to help brighten up the rather sombre bodystyles. This is the six cylinder 220 of 1954.

Below: It would be wrong to believe that this particular period was completely without style. The 300 range was aimed at restoring some of the Mercedes-Benz prestige. This model is significant for its pillarless body style, known as the panoramic-body.

220

Clever Compromise

The success of the comprehensive 170 range allowed Mercedes-Benz to introduce a new model range in the early 1950s. However, although economically things were beginning to improve, it is not surprising that the 220 was a development rather than a completely new model. Based on the successful 170s, the 220 was immediately recognisable from the now faired in headlights in the front fenders and the extensive use of chrome trimmings. If body and chassis were similar, the 220's major change was the use of the new six cylinder 2195cc engine developing 80bhp. By 1952, over 1000 per month were being made, a not inconsiderable achievement.

The range included two cabriolet versions; the A (two seater) and the B (a full five seater). The 220 Cabriolet B had a distinct resemblance to the Grosser Mercedes-Benz of the 1930s, but at a fraction of the price.

The 220 enjoyed good sales success in Germany, but export sales were limited and it was not exported to the United States. Those models that made it to Britain were very expensive and because of that won few friends.

A full range of commercial versions of the 220 were made in Germany as pick ups, ambulances and police cars.

300

Restoring Prestige

The 1951 Frankfurt Motor Show was a significant milestone for Mercedes-Benz as the unveiling of the 300 sedan showed not only the company's undoubted technical expertise but also its intention to get back into the luxury car market; a market that was just beginning to show signs of re-emerging in Germany. Good signs though they were, it was obvious that the 300 would have to have a good export sales market really to succeed and the Germany manufacturer's eyes were firmly set on the United States. It is no surprise, therefore, that the design had a strong American influence.

This was to be the car for the successful businessman and for Heads of State and the model got a great boost when it was used by the Federal German Government.

A backbone frame chassis in the now familiar Mercedes-Benz style was used with coil sprung swing axles at the rear and wishbone and coil independent at the front. One pointer to the future was that this car had electronically adjustable rear suspension to allow the driver to stiffen up the rear suspension when the car was under full load. Brakes were unassisted hydraulic ones, and rather marginal, requiring a great deal of pedal pressure.

Left, top and bottom: The Mercedes-Benz 300 range has to be one of the classics of the age. An imposing sight, the cabriolet versions attracted much attention with filmstars of the period. The S version (*bottom picture*) had a shortened wheelbase. All models were capable of 100mph top speed.

Right and below: The 180 models marked a significant milestone for Mercedes-Benz. These were the first models to move away from the separate chassis and body construction technique to the now commonplace monocoque construction. The one-piece chassis/body structure did limit the design — at least that's the only excuse this author can think of as they are rather dull.

Power was from the 2996cc six cylinder unit which had a fairly conventional cast iron block, light alloy cylinder head and chain driven camshaft. It was initially rated at 115bhp, and uprated to 125bhp in 1954. This was enough for 100mph top speed aided by its typically high gearing.

A shorter wheelbase version of the 300 chassis produced the 300S Cabriolet. An extremely elegant machine which featured a soft top that folded completely away out of sight to add to the vehicle's good looks. The car gained great fame when owned by the likes of Bing Crosby and Gary Cooper and Heads of State to the level of the Shah of Iran and King Hussein of Jordan.

180

Radical Departure
Up to the early 1950s all Mercedes-Benz models had the familiar backbone chassis, but the introduction of the 180 represented a radical departure from this and a move into what we recognise today as monocoque construction technique. Fritz Nallinger's engineering team designed a pressed-steel floor-pan stiffened in the center and welded to the body itself. This offered great torsional stiffness, less road noise and less overall weight.

The body style followed the trends of the day, and in this author's view, suffered because of that. Slab-sided and seemingly without much flair, it is one of the few Mercedes-Benz designs that travels time rather poorly.

The car kept the old side-valve 1767cc engine giving only 52bhp so it was

no sports car but was nevertheless set to become the most popular Mercedes-Benz of the 1950s.

The significance of the unitary construction design was developed throughout the 1950s, the model gaining the six cylinder engine and being designated the 220 in 1954. This model had a longer wheelbase which did much to improve the styling but also gave extra legroom in the rear.

The 220 cabriolet appeared in 1955 which is relatively soon after the model's launch given the difficulties involved with open-topped versions of unitary construction. This model was well enhanced with extra chrome side strips designed to brighten up the design.

220

The New Look
Thankfully, the trend for the rather bulbous body style went almost as soon as it came and the pressure was on Mercedes-Benz to produce a new range to meet the longer, low look being practised by the American stylists. This demand was met with the announcement of the 220 at the 1959 Frankfurt Show. The bulbous, rounded bodies did remain until 1961, but they were now joined by the new generation of design style from the German manufacturer, to be known affectionately by enthusiasts as the Fintail sedans. The body styles included the vertically stacked headlight arrangement that was to carry through for a number of years and contoured rear fins.

The fintail sedans were used by the company to promote the car's safety aspects as a marketing weapon — a ploy that had been started with the 180, the first unitary construction model.

A variety of engine options were available from the six cylinder in carburetor form to the fuel injected version that would propel the model to 107mph. Ride and handling were much improved on the 180 range although initially at least, the models only had drum brakes which was something of a handicap and a limitation that was corrected with the next fintail model to be launched.

300SE

Important Advance
The 300SE was a very advanced sedan. Introduced in 1961 it was based on the bodyshell of the 220 but with some important improvements. Despite the similarity, you could not mistake the 300SE because of the increased use of chrome work around the wheel-arches, down the waist line, and chromed

twin tail pipes. Powered by the fuel injected, 3-liter six cylinder the model had the self-levelling air suspension that previously had only been on the specialised 600 limousine, limited slip diff, hydraulic disc brakes, power steering and a new four speed automatic transmission.

The engine's 160bhp and the car's neat suspension propelled the vehicle at good speed and with remarkable smoothness. The cost of this comfortable and rapid progress, however, was its thirst for fuel. Indeed, when the car was announced it came with a 65-liter fuel tank, but this was found to be too small and was increased to 82 liters. But a thirst for fuel was not really to trouble those who could afford the comfort. Inside the car was well-appointed; wooden dashboard, central armrests front and rear, well upholstered seats. There were also the electrically lowered radio aerial and courtesy light delay that kept the light on for a period after the driver had got in – both these items were not to become common even on top class cars for another 20 years.

250S TO 300SEL

New Generation S-Class

One of the characteristics of the Mercedes-Benz model ranges is their comprehensive nature. It can at times be quite confusing checking all the different variations on a similar theme. The range that was introduced in 1965 was extremely comprehensive. The base 200 models kept the old bodystyle but the middle and upper range gained a revised body style, low waistline, curved side windows and the removal of the now dated rear fins.

The range was made all the more comprehensive and confusing due to emission control demands for the American cars. The S-class was originally intended to be a six-cylinder range only but a V8 had to be introduced and then that model specifically enlarged for the US market.

When the S-class was first advertised, Mercedes-Benz talked of the '38 new ideas' that had gone into the car but the new styling was the most signifi-

Left: Chrome was all the rage as Mercedes-Benz moved into the 1960s. This 300SE limousine is particularly well adorned with the add-on shine.

Above: Looking at this 1964 220SE you can spot the beginnings of a design philosophy that is very evident today. The SE, or coupe, versions of the Mercedes-Benz have a neat understated look; two doors and very clean lines especially the rear three-quarters.

Right: The 3-liter, fuel injected, six cylinder engine of the period was noted for its smoothness. Powering cars like the 220SE (*above*), the unit's 160bhp offered a good turn of speed.

The S-class model range was introduced in 1965 and was typical of Mercedes-Benz in being truly comprehensive. The base 200 models (*below and right*) kept the older body style and the extensive use of chrome while the others were a significant improvement. The 280 range was introduced in 1968 and included the 280SE Cabriolet (*left*) and the 280 SE Coupe (*below right*). As the designation suggests, these models were fitted with the then all new 2.8-liter six cylinder power unit.

cant difference. Larger glass area, bigger windshield and the lower coach line gave an illusion of much greater length. At the Frankfurt Show the first four S-class models were shown: 250S, 250SE, 300SE and 300SEL. All four models were luxuriously appointed and many observers commented that the L in the 300SEL designation obviously stood for Longer wheelbase. Mercedes-Benz always argued that despite this car having four extra inches, the L referred to the air suspension (*Luftfederung*) that replaced the standard springing.

In 1968 the range was increased with the all new 2.8-liter six cylinder to include the 280S, 280SE, 280SEL and 300SEL – and here the L did stand for 'long', this model not having the air suspension. Yes it gets confusing!

600 Pullman

Grosser, But Not Gross

Setting yourself the design brief to create the best passenger car in the world is obviously a tall order, it puts you up against Rolls-Royce in Great Britain and Cadillac in the United States. Whether Mercedes-Benz actually achieved that is an argument that will run and run, what is not disputed is that the 600 was one of the most awesome passenger cars of the time.

Work on the car was started in 1959 but it was not until the 1963 Paris Motor Show that the first car was shown and a further 12 months before production models were available. There were two different models; the 5/6 seater with its 126 in wheelbase and the 7/8 seater Pullman with 153.5 inch wheelbase. It was never called Grosser by the manufacturer (after the 1930s 770 sedan) but the epithet certainly suited the car. It was surely no coinci-

dence that at 20 ft 6 in, it was an inch longer than the Cadillac Fleetwood 75 Imperial Limousine – until the arrival of the 600, the longest production car in the world.

One of the surprising aspects of the 600's design was the fact that Mercedes-Benz engineers stuck with the unitary construction method for the car; both Cadillac and Rolls-Royce used separate body chassis units for their monster limos. The 600's front suspension instead was mounted on a detachable front subframe.

The car was powered by the 6332cc V8 engine which was the first production V8 from the company (not including racing engines). The engine produced a massive 300bhp at 4000rpm but at least 50bhp never made it to the rear wheels, being absorbed instead by all the additional engine-driven systems; air conditioning, compressor for the brakes, steering and air suspension. Despite this diversion of power, the 2.5-ton machine could be pro-

pelled at speeds up to 130mph. Understandably, it would consume fuel at a serious rate, 10mpg being a good average.

All kinds of electronic gadgetry was fitted as standard. Electrically raised and lowered windows, central locking, electrically adjustable front and rear seats were all extras that are now familiar but very special in 1963 – even the spare wheel rested on a large spring which raised it to a more convenient position should you, or more likely your chauffeur, have to change a flat. In this area, the 600 did have an advantage in that all these engine-driven compressor systems were completely silent which is not what could be said of some of the Rolls and Cadillac electric servos of the time.

A wide variety of models was built. An extra set of doors in the middle did not cause any structural rigidity problems. The State Landaulet 600 had a fold down portion on the rear third of the roof to allow for the public to see the passengers clearly during official parades.

The Grosser Mercedes-Benz just has to be one of the most awesome passenger cars built. The German company set out to create a better limousine than either Rolls-Royce or Cadillac and the result is truly impressive. Always known by the manufacturer as the 600, these limousines were powered by the 6.3-liter V8 engine which – racing engines apart – was the first production V8 built by the company. The model shown *left*, obviously has presidential aspirations, but it was possible to have a shorter wheelbase version for more private usage (*right*).

Below: The success of the 6.3-liter V8 engine in the 600 range led Mercedes-Benz to install the unit in the 300 bodyshell. The result was a performance sedan, the like of which had not really been known before; the 300 SEL 6.3 had a 0 to 60mph time of only 6.5 seconds and a top speed of 137mph. In Europe it was voted Car of the Year.

Always built to order, only 2677 were completed. Few ever made it to Great Britain, especially after the new Rolls-Royce Silver Shadow appeared in 1965. The car was far more popular in the United States. Orders dropped off considerably after the 1973 fuel crisis and then American emission controls prevented its sale across the Atlantic. Production ceased in 1981.

300SEL 6.3

Power Surprise

The 1968 Geneva Show saw a surprise on the Mercedes-Benz stand in the shape of a standard 300 bodyshell. Under the hood was shoe-horned the 6.3-liter V8 from the 600 limousine. Surprisingly, perhaps, few modifications were necessary to squeeze the large power unit into the space. The car was a real wolf in sheep's clothing, a comfortable family sedan one moment and a real road burner the next, with a 0-60mph in only 6.5 seconds and a top speed of 137mph.

The car was the idea of Erich Waxenberger of Mercedes-Benz experimental department and it is rumored that he fitted the engine as a surprise and let his bosses drive the car without telling them what he had done! All the torque available meant that the car had to have the four speed automatic gearbox from the 600 limousine. The performance was good enough, however, for the respected American motoring magazine *Road & Track* to describe the car as 'merely the greatest sedan in the world'. The American emission controls finally put an end to its US sales, while in Europe it was voted Car of the Year by a number of motoring publications.

Only 6526 were built and it must rank as one of the great sedans of the 1960s; muscular and luxurious, power with style.

450 SEL

Top Of The Range

1972 saw the introduction of two new super efficient twin-cam six-cylinder engines designed to meet American emission laws. The engine was first placed into existing sedans and coupes before being included in a completely new range of S-class sedans. Much of the work for this S-class range had been done on the C111 experimental vehicles (see Chapter Five). The body style showed a strong family resemblance to other models in the range – a trait which has been continued to this very day.

Elegant rather than stunning, these S-class models all had completely new running gear with double wishbone suspension at the front with zero offset steering (developed on the C111). At the rear the swing axle set-up, for so long the standard Mercedes-Benz arrangement, gave way to semi-trailing arm. The choice of transmission was five speed manual or automatic on the six cylinder cars, with a new three speed automatic for the 200bhp V8 models.

In 1973, the range was increased to include the 450 series, models fitted with the 4.5-liter V8. This model was a huge success and rightly acclaimed. It was described by one prominent journal at the time as 'the very pinnacle of passenger car development.' It was voted Car of the Year in Europe.

There was little visual difference between the 450SEL and the more modest models in the range but the car's performance and high level of equipment certainly made it stand out from the crowd. It would accelerate to 60mph in around 9 seconds and would top 130mph with ease. Although the 600 limousine was still available at the time, that was a specialist hand-built car, and the 450SEL was very comfortably top of the Mercedes-Benz stable. No question.

T-Series

Entering The Space Age

Quite why Mercedes-Benz took so long to build a station wagon version is puzzling. Specialists had been converting Mercedes-Benz sedans for some years before the company was to do the job itself in 1978. History has shown that immediately after the Second World War, many Mercedes-Benz sedans were built in various commercial styles – ambulances, delivery vans, pick-ups – and one can but assume that the company felt relieved to have climbed away from that past and established itself in the luxury sedan field so that it didn't 'need' a station wagon.

Left: The 450 SEL of 1972 is significant in that it was powered by the twin-cam six cylinder engines that had been designed specifically to meet American emission regulations.

Right and below: Mercedes-Benz took an awful long while before building a station wagon. One can only assume that the company looked on the vehicles as too much like the commercials they had been forced to produce immediately after the Second World War just to keep in business. The basic looks of the T-series have received high praise, however. All the models here use diesel engines.

As one would expect, however, when the decision was made, the job was done very comprehensively. Production started at Bremen in the old Borgward factory which had been taken over in 1971. The aim was to make a range that drove and handled like the sedan versions on which they were based, both when empty and when fully laden. To accommodate this, a special self-levelling rear suspension was designed and fitted. An engine driven hydraulic pump compensates for weight in the rear and stiffens up the shock absorbers accordingly.

Various T-series models have been made, based on sedan equivalents. Mercedes-Benz introduced turbocharged diesel models to the range after 1979, produced with both economy and the emission requirements of America very much to the fore. Very popular in Europe have been the turbo-diesel variants of the T-series; economical space wagons with all the creature comforts of top class sedans.

1980 S-Class

Into The Eighties

The innate conservatism of the Mercedes-Benz styling department — generally a trait that seems widespread throughout German motor manufacturers — was highlighted with the launch of the 1980 S-class range. At first, even second glance, the cars looked little changed beside their predecessors, perhaps just a minor revamp of the older models. However, looks can be deceiving because this was a completely new vehicle. Narrower and longer, the designers had paid great attention to the car's aerodynamics as well as reducing the car's overall weight. The result was a claimed 10 percent fuel saving. A useful claim for a company producing quality sedans to be seen concentrating on fuel economy.

The first models introduced were the carburetor 280S, fuel injected 280SE, 380SE, 500SE (with longer wheelbase SEL versions on the last three).

One of the major developments with this S-class range was the debut of the alloy V8. Available in both 3.8 and 5.0-liter sizes they were lighter and more efficient, producing 204 and 231bhp respectively, both using Bosch K-Jetronic fuel injection. It was an impressive package all round and was to stand Mercedes-Benz in good order for the next ten years.

Left: The original 1979 T-series Mercedes-Benz station wagon models were well received, but really became desirable vehicles in their own right with the revamped ranges in the mid-1980s (*above*). These later designs show a much improved body style and considerably less chrome.

Right: The 1980 S-class designs once again highlighted the innate conservatism in the Mercedes-Benz styling department. This is the 280 version, and looks very similar to the 380 and 500 models.

Left: Two door versions of the Mercedes-Benz range have always been available and the 1983 380 and 500SEC models were no exception. Looking at the two models parked together emphasises that the only significant differences were under the hood.

Right: The 380 SEC must be regarded as one of the nicest looking Mercedes-Benz of the period. Powered by the 3.8-liter V8 the car offered 130mph performance and acceleration to match.

Below: The 500 SEL of 1983 was a big car. Despite this, however, it was no slouch. A 0 to 60 mph time in 8 seconds is impressive by any standards, for a car that weighs 3900 pounds it is quite an achievement.

380SEC

Fuel Conscious Coupe

Mercedes-Benz has always offered two door coupe versions of its model range and the introduction of the S-class cars of the 1980s led to perhaps one of the nicest versions of this theme with the 380SEC. This car has the 3839cc version of the V8 engine delivering 204bhp and offering over 130mph top speed and 0-60mph acceleration in just over 9 seconds. It is surprising, therefore, to read contemporary accounts of this car where the performance seems to take second place to the company's 'Energy Concept' and the outstanding fuel economy achieved by the 380SEC!

As we have explained, the S-class of the eighties placed a high emphasis on fuel economy but without any major losses in performance or quality appeal. The 380SEC is, therefore, a very impressive machine. The pillarless bodyshape is clean and attractive, the performance as you would expect and, despite only being a two door, the car is capable of carrying four adults in comfort.

The model had a high export price but a strong appeal for the market of coupe enthusiasts which is big in both Great Britain and the United States.

500SEL

Big Boy

For a car that is nearly 17ft long and weighing almost 3900 pounds, you could be forgiven for thinking this is a tank-like limousine that would be great to be driven in, but not much fun actually to drive. On the contrary, however, this is a good example of a model that while large and extremely well appointed is actually very satisfying to drive. The all-alloy 4973cc, 231bhp power unit is well capable of propelling the big car to over 130mph and up to 60mph in an impressive 8.0 seconds. The engine is also technically interesting in that, despite being all-alloy, Mercedes-Benz has done away with the need for cast iron liners for the cylinder bores. A clever method of etching and coating the aluminum cylinder bores actually prevents the excessive wear which normally necessitates cast iron liners for an aluminum block.

The engine's dynamic characteristics are not unlike a big American V8, delivering the power in a smooth leisurely manner, seemingly very docile until the driver floors that right foot.

As you would expect, standard equipment levels are high and include air conditioning, anti-lock braking, cruise control, limited-slip differential, central locking, electric window lifts, headlight wash/wipe and tinted glass.

190

Thinking Smaller

The 190 Mercedes-Benz introduced at the end of 1982 is probably the most significant car from this manufacturer in the past two or even three decades. There is nothing particularly significant technically about the design; there is nothing particularly stunning about the visual style either. The significant thing about the 190 is its size – or rather lack of it.

This was described as the 'baby Mercedes-Benz' and a response to what the manufacturer saw as a world-wide trend for smaller cars, 'down-sizing' as it is also known. All things are relative, of course, and what is small for Mercedes-Benz is really just medium sized for other more modest standards. The wheelbase of the 190 is 110 inches and there had not been a similar sized Mercedes-Benz since the 180 back in the 1950s. It is understandable, therefore, that while rumors about the car existed for a number of years (the company instituted a design study to be established back in 1974), there was a long gestation before the baby was actually born.

When it did arrive, it looked a lot like its brothers and sisters, the marked family resemblance adding to the difficulties of telling the difference between models at anything but close range. Under the skin, it took the company's smallest engine, the 1997cc four cylinder that had been introduced into the 200 range in 1980. The major technical interest came from the rear suspension which had abandoned the trailing arm set-up to go for an unusual five link system with unequal length wishbone geometry.

The aim with the car was to appeal to a completely new market, a younger market, that would not normally consider a Mercedes-Benz for reasons of both price and image. Indeed, although the 190 was a down-sized car, the price in export markets like Britain remain quite high in comparison with its competitors. Certainly this was not an attempt to produce a 'Merc for the masses' but it was set to make a significant increase numerically in cars sold by the German manufacturer.

190E 2.3-16

Back From The Track

If the standard 190 is a relatively bland visual design, then the same cannot be said for the exciting 2.3-16. The serious body kit of side skirts, front air dam and neat, almost cheeky rear wing tell a rather different story. The designation of 2.3-16 tells rather more; the 2.3-liter four cylinder engine is a multi-valve unit with 16 valves in place. And it is with the cylinder head that the interesting link between the German company and the highly respected British concern of Cosworth Engineering becomes apparent.

When Mercedes-Benz decided to produce a sporty version to top the 190 range, and a car that would be eligible to meet the regulations for European touring car racing, it contracted Cosworth to work on the engine. It is not that

Mercedes-Benz could not have done the job 'in-house' but more sensibly the economies of scale made a contract with a specialist more logical. The car was always going to have a limited annual production run – around 7000 – and so joining forces with Cosworth was obvious. But don't expect to see any Cosworth badges anywhere on the car!

The result of this collaboration is a four cylinder engine that produces 185bhp at 6200rpm with that power transmitted through a five speed box. The car sits some 15mm lower with stiffer dampers and thicker anti-roll bars. In road-going trim, the chassis is actually capable of handling more power, a sensible attribute as it means positive performance on the road with the car able to be developed on the track to go even quicker.

When driving the car, the performance seems just a shade subdued. It will reach 145mph top speed, but the 0-60mph spring takes around 8 seconds, competent for a car of that size and weight but not quite a match for those overtly aggressive looks. The car was also hampered with an extremely heavy retail price but then as it was always to be a limited production run, was well built and dynamically excellent to drive. Add this to the special ingredient of having an engine developed with Cosworth and that price begins to make a little more sense.

1985 560SEL

Enter The Big Cats

The revised S-class range of 1985 once again showed Mercedes-Benz's commitment to emission controls. Pressure was growing in Germany at this time to cut down air pollution and Mercedes-Benz wanted to be ready for the time when the fitting of catalytic converters became mandatory. The changes to the S-class were, therefore, predominantly under the skin rather than on the visual side.

The significant changes were to the bore and stroke of the all-aluminum V8 engines, changing the sizes to 5547cc and 4196cc. The 560 engine produces 300bhp and is fitted with the four speed automatic transmission. This transmission has the addition of a Sport or Economy mode allowing the driver to select either performance or fuel efficient motoring.

The 560SEL also has hydropneumatic suspension and height adjustment. A flick of the switch changes the car's suspension from the normal 'softer' ride to a firmer, crisper handling package ideal for high speed maneuvers. The height adjustment has been designed to lower the car when it is travelling at speeds above 120kmph (75mph), reducing the aerodynamic drag of the body and gaining better fuel consumption. This may seem rather elaborate, but on a long autobahn journey the corresponding fuel saving can be quite significant.

Despite the 560SEL weighing 3990lb it will top 145mph with ease and sprint from a standing start to 60mph in just under 8 seconds which shows the power of the V8 engine.

In 1982, Mercedes-Benz had a baby! At the time, much was made of this new, small, Mercedes. However, as we can see from the company's history, smaller cars had played a part in the marque's success. The 190 continued that success. It was introduced when all manufacturers were 'down-sizing'. Visually the 190 was hardly inspiring (*top left*) although the sporting version built with help in the engine bay from British tuning expert Cosworth, in the form of the 2.3-16 (*left*) did help the car's image.

Right: For the 1985 redesign of the S-class, catalytic convertors were fitted to the V8 engine. Other changes to the range were predominantly under the skin, visually the car was instantly recognisable as a Mercedes-Benz.

Left and above: Once again, the updated 1989 range saw only minor external changes. The molded side skirts were the most significant and can be clearly seen on all three models from the 300 range shown here.

Right: Compared to the conservative image of the 300 series, the 2.5-16 looks positively outrageous . . .

300E and SE-24

Mid-Range Masterpiece

If you have been reading this book from the beginning it will not surprise you that the 1989 changes to the mid-range Mercedes-Benz models, the 300s, were minor on the outside but major under the skin. Visually the major changes were to the molded side skirts which became far smoother than on previous models and keyed to the car's body color. That was a subtle but extremely attractive development

The major importance, however, is to the new 24-valve 3-liter straight six engine. Already an option on the superb SL sports cars (see Chapter Three) they were put into service in the sedan, coupe and estate 300s from this date. The four valve per cylinder-head unit develops 220bhp and offers sparkling performance. The engine also has an impressive positive function towards exhaust emissions. This range, as with all German cars, is fitted with the mandatory catalytic converter. However, one of the limitations of the 'cat' is that it needs to reach a certain temperature before it works efficiently. Cold starts, therefore, still see high levels of harmful exhaust emissions. On this engine, a cold start procedure supplies fresh air downstream of the exhaust valves where it reacts with the exhaust gases to cause a chemical reaction which increases the temperature and contributes to getting the 'cat' up to its working temperature much sooner.

Mercedes-Benz models from this date are also available with the company's Sportsline suspension packages. It is possible for buyers to select stiffer suspension if they wish to have a sportier handling package. On the 300CE-24, the Sportsline package produces an excellent sporting coupe with a great deal more character for the enthusiastic driver to enjoy than would be possible with earlier versions of this model – a big plus point.

190E 2.5 – 16 Evolution II

Winged Wonder

OK, how do you tell the difference between the 1989 190E 2.5-16 which replaced the 190E 2.3-16? Why the chrome number 5 on the trunklid, what else did you expect? The actual change had as much to do with a desire for more power on the race track as it did for giving the car the extra urge on the road that it always deserved.

Engine capacity was increased to 2498cc by increasing the stroke. The multi-valve cylinder head remained as the original model but a change of camshafts saw the power increased to 197bhp at 6200rpm. In pure acceleration times it brought the 0-60mph sprint down to just over 7 seconds which was much more respectable. Top speed remained much as before at just over 140mph.

The other significant change was the use of the fitting of the Mercedes-Benz hi-tech limited slip rear differential. This is an electronically controlled and hydraulically operated differential that can vary the locking effect of the rear wheels between 35 and 100 percent. The advantage here is for when the car is being driven hard in a corner and one rear wheel lifts or just loses traction and the sensors ensure that more power goes to the wheel with more grip. Good for spirited road driving but also a distinct advantage for the motorsporting arena.

It is purely to suit the motorsporting regulations that the awesome Evolution II version was introduced in 1990. The amazing rear wing aids the high speed handling on the track. The larger air dam under the front bumper has two positions; one, very low, for high speed touring and racing, with the second setting being much higher to allow for driving around town without the ignominy of scraping one's nose on the floor. But perhaps the far more significant aspects are the larger wheel and tire combination which, as well as helping racing grip, actually permits the use of bigger brakes, another competitive bonus. Subtle changes to the engine specification have also all been made to allow for more radical tuning when the car hits the race track. This is now a very special 190, a long way from the original concept of the smaller car, but Touring Car Racing (as the competition is called in Europe

where these cars are eligible) is big business and is networked on satellite television. When Mercedes-Benz sedans are doing well on the track this is usually reflected by sales in the showrooms. The 190E 2.5-6 Evolution II is quite a flagship and, unusual for a Mercedes-Benz, very easy to spot, even at a distance.

500E

Exclusive Express

The 500E is the fastest accelerating road-going car ever produced by Mercedes-Benz. It is also one of the most exclusive with only 12 of these cars built each day off a special production line manned by trained craftsmen. The car is actually built in Porsche's Zuffenhausen factory a few miles away from the main Mercedes-Benz plant in Stuttgart. Porsche has been involved with the development of the car, and this is, of course, not the first time that the companies have been linked, as Ferdinand Porsche was head of design before Daimler joined with Benz back in 1926.

Powered by the 32-valve 5-liter V8 and producing 326bhp, this imposing sedan is capable of reaching 62mph in under six seconds and like other high performance Mercedes-Benz models is governed to a 155mph maximum speed. This is the engine in the 500SL sports car and to fit into the 500E – which is based on the 300E bodyshell – changes have had to be made to the engine compartment.

Visually, only the smart alloy wheels and discreet wheel arch extensions give away any indication of the car's performance potential. But it is under the skin that the real technological excitement lies. The 500E has the latest form of electronic engine management control system to limit the top speed and the anti-skid control (ASR) to prevent wheel spin or the loss of grip. No matter what the driver does, or what the road surface is, the electronic brain will immediately respond to the potential of a slipping wheel and reduce power accordingly.

The 500E also has what Mercedes-Benz has claimed is a world first. All the electronic control functions on the car are collected into a 'data bus' system and constantly communicate with each other. For example, when the ASR system recognises a situation where the wheels are about to slip and therefore reduces the power to those wheels, the 'data bus' system relays that information to the engine, altering the ignition timing and the fuel injection unit to save fuel. In short, the sensors all over the 500E 'talk' to one another.

Stretching Into The Future

Although not announcing it as the return of the famous 600 range, 1990 did see the return of the factory-built stretched limousine. Based on the mid-range body style and running gear, the limousine has an extra 800mm in the middle which is enough for an extra pair of doors and allows the car to carry eight adults in comfort. The vehicle is available with either the diesel engine from the 250D model or the 2.6-liter gasoline version. Production will be limited, with once again, cars built specifically to order.

Left: Who said Mercedes-Benz models all look the same . . . ? This has to be one of the most striking cars in the book, the Evolution II version of the 2.5-16 190. The huge rear wing, extended wheel arches, side skirts and massive wheel and tire combination were all necessitated for this model to participate in the German Touring Car Championship.

Below: The return of the 600 series? No, not quite. This is a limited production stretched limousine based on the mid-range models.

As this book is being written, more news is filtering from Stuttgart about future models. One magazine has even shown scoop photographs of the new 190 range; longer, wider and considerably more rounded in styling than its predecessor, the baby of the range looks well set to come of age. There is also talk of a Sports Kombi version, a two door 190 with a longer roof line that doesn't quite make the car a station-wagon but makes it more than just another coupe. A bold new initiative from Mercedes-Benz that is for sure.

What is also sure is the forthcoming revision to the S-class range which this time will include a V12 engine. The 600SEC will push the boundaries of luxurious performance motoring even further. Bristling with sophisticated electronic systems the car will be a technical enthusiast's dream. In some respects, however, Mercedes-Benz is behind its main rivals like Jaguar and BMW, both of whom have got V12 versions in their ranges. This means the engine and the vehicle it is fitted to, will be up against tough opposition, but you wouldn't bet against it being a success.

Built To Stun

Individual Mercedes-Benz conversions
It has to be said that there is a strong underlying vein of conservatism within the Stuttgart manufacturer. Without a doubt, the company is dedicated to technical advancement, engineering excellence and unerring build quality.

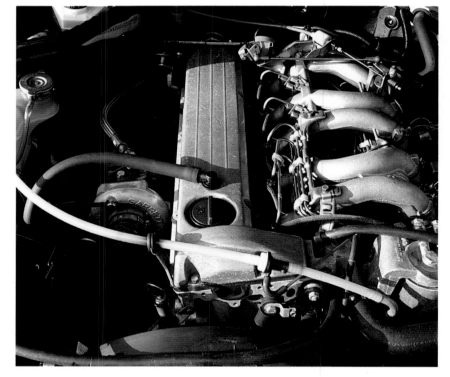

Top: The Mercedes-Benz passenger train. The stretched limousine announced in 1990 will carry six people in a high degree of comfort.

Above and left: Mercedes-Benz have always had some success with diesel models. This is the 300, powered by the six cylinder, 155bhp turbo diesel engine.

Above right: A number of specialist companies produce conversions on standard models. This is a 300 series converted by Brabus; body kit, lowered suspension and imposing wheels and tires complete the picture.

But it is not flash. With the sole exception of the 190 Evolution II which has been built to meet the necessary motorsporting regulations, there is no product on the entire range, that has been built to be ostentatious. Those in the know, know the quality, so why shout about it?

Well this is not the place to investigate the human pysche, but there are people who want to be flash, brash, loud and individualistic. If Mercedes-Benz believe that they build the best engineered, highest quality, luxury, performance sedans in the world, there are people who want more, and there are other people prepared to − try − and give it to them.

These are the conversion specialists, the expensive end of the motoring aftermarket business that will build you a car that they can almost guarantee is individualistic enough to make it supremely unlikely that you will ever see another one like it.

It is here that we enter a world where taste becomes a very personal matter indeed and price, far from being no object, seems actively encouraged to be high as it merely helps to reinforce the claimed uniqueness of the product.

There are a small number of engineering concerns that take the standard Mercedes-Benz product and transform it into quite another machine altogether; these are Mercs for extroverts.

AMG is a well established engineering and design facility located at Affalterbach, quite close to Stuttgart and it is here that Mercedes-Benz models are transformed both inside and out into an unmistakably radical roadburner. On the outside, a full body-kit is fitted; deeper front air dam, lower side skirts and rear spoiler where before there were none. It is unmistakably 'add-on' in its appearance, but not because you can see the join where plastic meets metal, but because you just *know* that this is not a standard car, this is different. The car will sit lower too, with new suspension settings and bigger wheels but with ultra low profile tires.

Inside the car expect the same approach. Gone are the standard seats to have been covered by a rarer leather cloth, buffalo hide is the most likely. Out will go the standard car's walnut dash and door cappings to be replaced with a rarer even more heavily lacquered variety.

But it is under the hood that the real changes are made. A company like AMG could not have built its reputation on a cleverly fitted set of party clothes, you need to match the pose with the performance. AMG's options here include the completely re-engineered 3-liter six cylinder that has a longer throw crankshaft, lightweight pistons and increased capacity to 3205cc. AMG's own camshaft profile keeps the valves open just that little bit longer which raises the output from the factory's already impressive 188bhp to a staggering 245bhp at 5750rpm.

A standard 300CE, fitted with the aforementioned body-kit, suspension and power busting engine will rocket from standstill to 100mph in only 19 seconds and on and on to a top speed of 146mph.

But that is not where it ends. If that is not enough, AMG will shoe-horn their own 6-liter version of the Mercedes-Benz 32-valve V8 under the same 300CE bonnet. This engine's power output is a claimed 400bhp − only a decade ago that was the power offered by Formula One GP cars. We are now talking about the 0-60mph dash in under 5 seconds and a top speed said to be 180mph.

This comes with a price tag, of course, likely to be over 200,000Dm, but you won't see another one like it in your street.

But AMG is not alone, in the small town of Bottrop, near Dusseldorf is where the delightfully named Bodo Buschmann runs Brabus Autosport where, for similarly impressive price tags, he has on offer tuned and converted Mercedes-Benz models. If there is a difference it is perhaps that Brabus is less outrageous with the body kits, happier that the underhood engineering and interior styling will suffice to attract that specialist buyer. When it comes to the engineering, the head of engineering at Brabus has come direct from the Mercedes-Benz technical department.

When it comes to changes to the styling, Lorinser make a range of Mercedes-Benz body-kits that are of the highest order and to this author's eyes the most pleasing options of all those mentioned. When you take a car of such obvious style and class as the 500SL sports car and add a body kit you had better know what you are doing. The result from Lorinser seems to indicate that they do.

And how does the mother company respond to these developments? They are not frowned upon, but one suspects they are not enthused about either. Tolerated might be the better description. In the case of AMG, the association is at its closest, as the conversion specialist works closely with Mercedes-Benz on its racing program. Much of the work on the awesome 190E 2.5-16 Evolution II has been done in association with AMG and that alone is quite a recommendation. AMG also helped with the initial Group C sports prototype car (see Chapter Four).

Not perhaps to everyone's taste, and certainly not to everyone's budget, the converted Mercedes-Benz is nevertheless a real head turner.

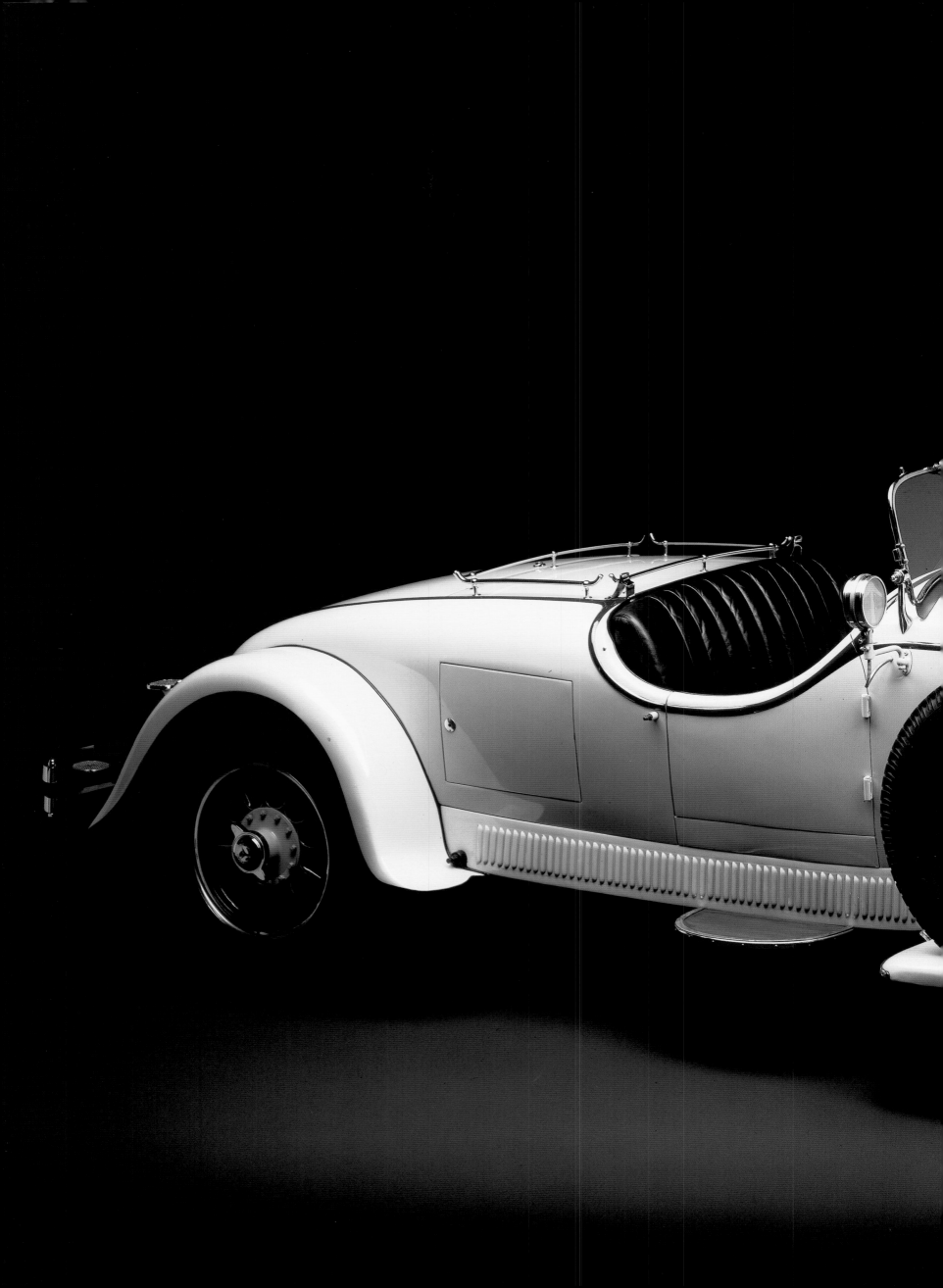

Sports Time

Yes, Mercedes-Benz has made some good sedans. But the real style, the class, the passion that is so much the natural ingredient when discussing things automotive has to be a manufacturer's sports cars. And these are the stars of the three-pointed star. No question.

What is a sports car? People have different views on that subject, that's for sure. Early English ones related to a car that it was impossible to get into without removing one's hat, to the American version which was that a sports car was one where the seats folded down to make beds. Since I am the author of this book, you are going to be stuck with my definition; a sports car is a performance package that offers the person behind the wheel a unique experience of driving pleasure. Sports cars must excite, they must have character. Often, but not always, they are open-topped. Sports cars are special.

Mention has to be made about whether they are open-topped because if you go back to the very beginning of the automobile's history, the first horse-less carriages were all open-topped yet they were hardly sports cars! On the other side of the coin, the Mercedes-Benz range includes one particular model which has a fixed roof yet remains one of the most famous sports cars of all. But more of that later.

Back in the 1920s, it was a regular feature for manufacturers to offer a sports version of most models in the range. Manufacturers had fewer models in their range, of course, and it was rather easier to offer a shorter chassis, lighter, slightly more powerful version and call it the "Sports". It would be wrong to chronicle all of these, but with Mercedes-Benz it is fair to start immediately after the amalgamation of Daimler and Benz and the era of the big, blown sports cars.

Previous page: The start of the super sports. This 1926 Mercedes 600 was built the year of the amalgamation between Benz and Daimler. The superb lines and side-mounted spare wheel, so typical of the period, still turn heads today.

Right: This was the era of the supercharged sports car. At the time these cars were the pinnacle of motoring technology. This example is a 1927 SSK and had a power output of 225bhp – and remember this is the mid-1920s.

Below: The sporting nature of the period also produced some excellent four seater cabriolets. This is a 1926 Type 28/95 with a 7-liter six cylinder power unit.

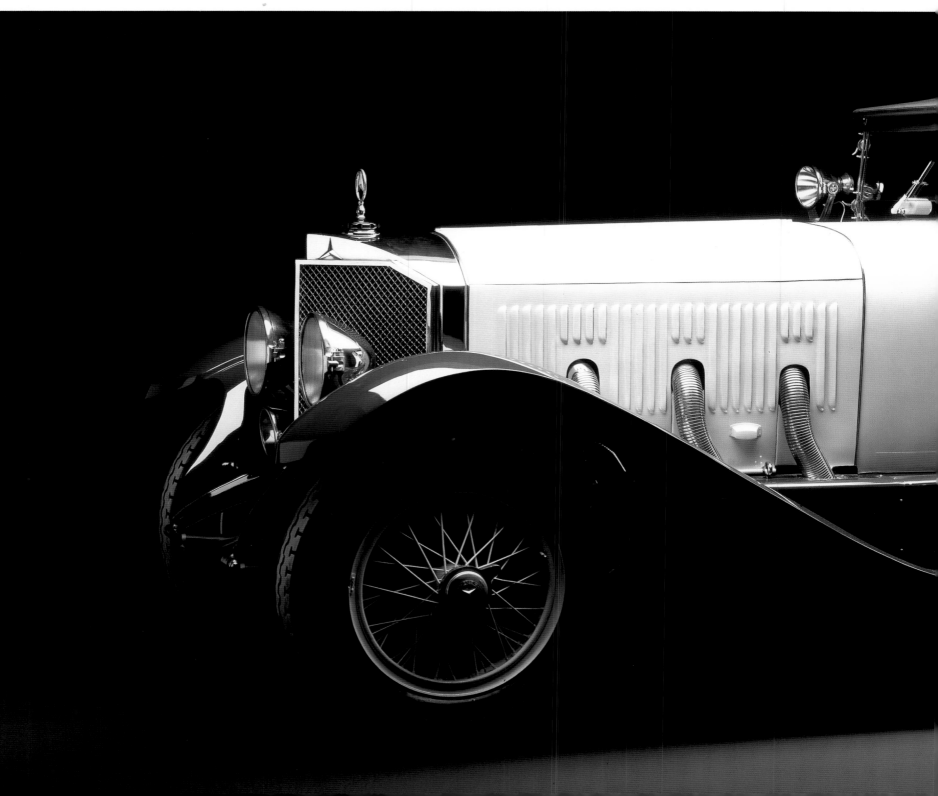

These great supercharged sports cars built from 1926 onwards were certainly the pinnacle of performance motoring. The 1926 K was a shortened version of the 170 sedan. Its 6.25-liter six cylinder engine produced 160bhp at only 2600rpm thanks to the supercharger and it could top 100mph. Stopping the thing was rather different, however, and it gained a rather unenviable reputation owing to very poor brakes.

The K was replaced by the S (for Sport) a year later. Now with an enlarged engine and 180bhp, changes to the chassis improved the handling but still the brakes were the model's weakest point. Although neither of these models was a pure racing machine, they took many notable victories at the time in the hands of the highly talented Rudolf Caracciola.

The model was developed through the SS (Super Sports) in 1928 (7.1-liter, 225bhp) and then the SSK (Super Sports Short), a lighter version which still looks as good and imposing today as it did 60 years ago.

In the early 1930s, the design of the Mercedes-Benz sports car moved into perhaps its most graceful era with the announcement of the fabulous 500K. This magnificent machine was most definitely the supercar of its day. The supercharged, 5-liter, straight eight engine under the six foot long hood delivered 160bhp when the Roots-type supercharger was engaged. The sweeping lines of the fenders matched with the glorious slope of the tail cannot fail to move any automobile enthusiast. The 540K followed, the engine size now increased to 5.4 liters. These were superb sports cars, limited in production number due to the Depression and the onset of the Second World War; they were the last of the decadent, performance monsters.

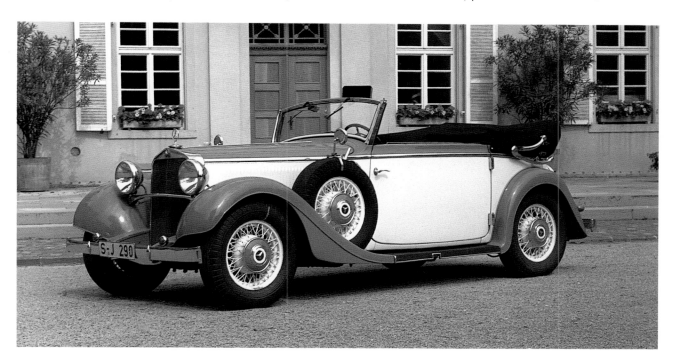

Left: This rather bizarre looking machine was actually ahead of its time. Based on the short-lived rear engined 130 sedan, this sports version had the 55bhp overhead camshaft engine in the mid-engined position. Built in 1935 it was known as the Type 150.

Below: The 540K followed the initial success of the 500K. The straight eight engine was supercharged and delivered 160bhp. There is a spare wheel fitted each side of the pontoon fenders. Superb machines.

Right: Three liter cabriolets were popular in the mid 1930s. This is the 290 Cabriolet C of 1933.

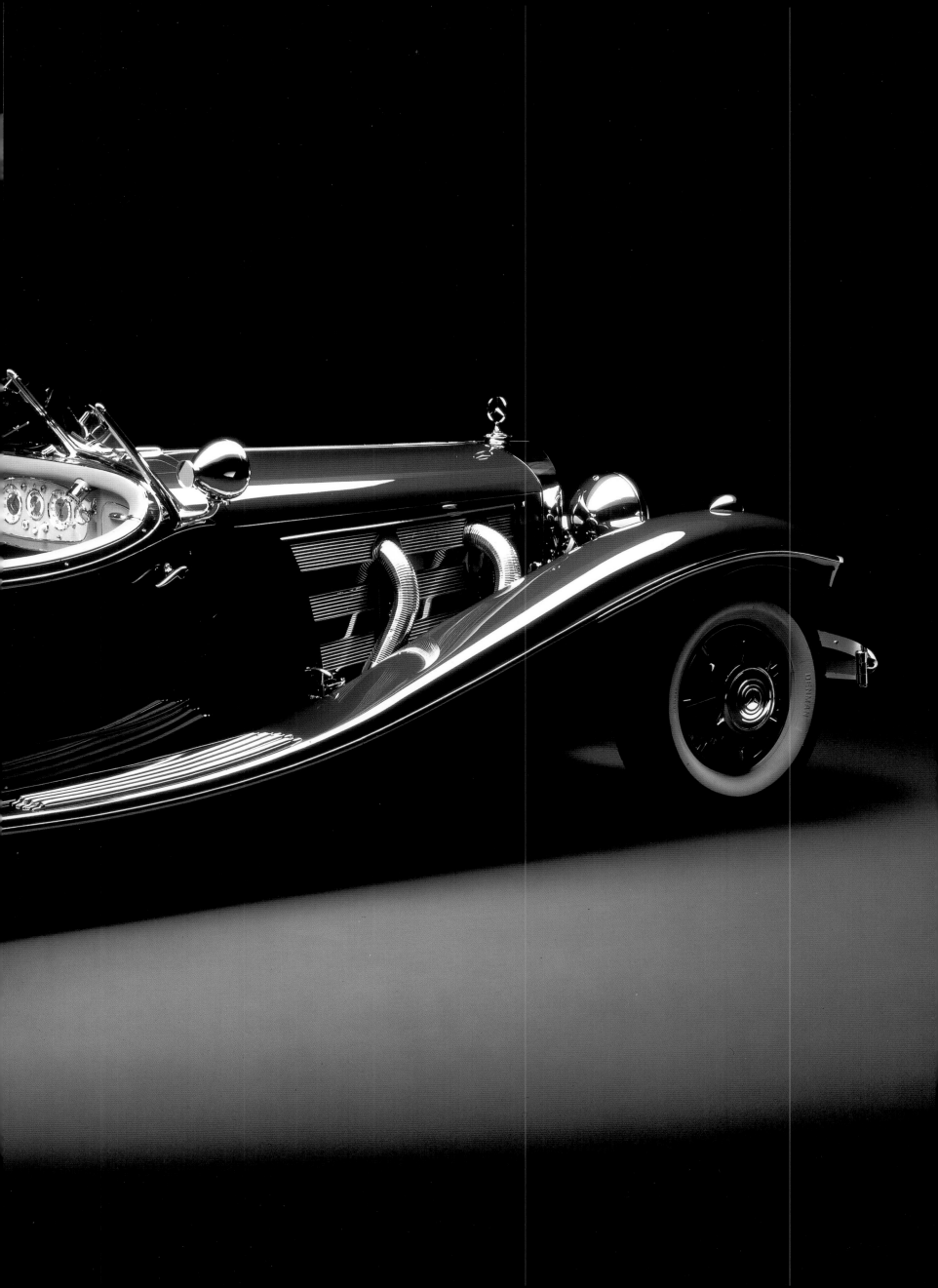

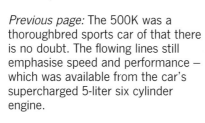

Previous page: The 500K was a thoroughbred sports car of that there is no doubt. The flowing lines still emphasise speed and performance – which was available from the car's supercharged 5-liter six cylinder engine.

Top left and above: The 'Gullwing' Mercedes-Benz has to be one of the most instantly recognisable cars ever built. Derived directly from the competition 300SL of 1952, the road version arrived two years later.

Left: The 300 SL Roadster followed the 'Gullwing' and somehow lacks the panache of the closed coupe version.

The Modern Age

As we have explained, before the Second World War, the Mercedes-Benz racing program had for a while been based on the sports cars that were being built on the main production line. In other words, in the 1920s and early 1930s, the company raced what was available, until the purpose built racing department took over and built pure race cars. After the war, however, things were the other way around. The 300SL was built as the re-entry vehicle for the company into motor racing, and from that came one of the world's most famous sports cars.

The 300SL (Sports Leicht : light) started production as a road car in 1954, a couple of years after the racing versions as a direct reaction to the demand from America for a road version of the successful racing car. Its small coupe body shape featured the now famous gullwing doors, necessary because of the lightweight spaceframe chassis that prevented 'normal' doors running low enough to be of any use. A tilting steering wheel was also part of the specification to allow for ease of entry and exit.

The major development with the road cars was the introduction of Bosch fuel injection for the six-cylinder engine raising the power output to 215bhp, which was actually considerably more than the race cars. With the highest available rear axle ratio, the top speed of the 300SL was actually 160mph, extremely impressive for a 1954 road car.

The Gullwing Mercedes-Benz was so-called because of its distinctive doors. These were not just a gimmick, however, but a necessity due to the car's tubular spaceframe chassis. The chassis was based directly on the racing 300SL. The six cylinder 2996cc engine propelled the car to a top speed in excess of 160mph, which for a 1955 sports car was performance indeed. The Gullwing was a great success in promoting the company name that Mercedes-Benz decided to make a rather more conventional sports car in 1957 – the 300 SL Roadster. This car proved so popular it remained in production until 1963.

For those who did not want the 'gullwing' doors, there was a roadster version launched in 1957 which remained in production until 1963.

Much like the 500K before it, the price of the 300SL – it was over £4000 in Britain in 1954 – limited its volume and made it a sports car only for the very well heeled. The low volume has also ensured the model's value on the classic car market today. The high price was, of course, due to the car's racing heritage, the spaceframe chassis was more expensive to produce in any great number than using a 'normal' chassis. The impressive public reaction to the car, however, made the idea of a cheaper sports car a natural next step for Mercedes-Benz.

The high demand was met by the 190SL. The styling reflected the 300SL, but it was based on the chassis of the 180 sedan and it was powered by that model's four cylinder 105bhp engine. The 180 sedan handled well enough but the 190SL looked a better sports car than it actually was.

The 190SL is, therefore, close to not being included in my definition of sports car as it appeared something of a sports fraud. It served a purpose, though, in that it highlighted a demand. Mercedes-Benz recognised this and replaced it with a significantly different look in 1963 when the 230SL was introduced at the Geneva Show. This was rather a better compromise. The unique 'pagoda' style hard-top roof line certainly meant that it turned heads but now with the 2.3-liter, fuel injected six cylinder, performance was there to match the looks. There were some who thought this was not a sports car because it was available with automatic transmission and power steering, but it is fair to say that this was the start of a new breed of sports car – Mercedes-Benz were ahead of the game here as they recognised that a sports car need not be short on luxury. The 'L' in the SL designation can from now on be more accurately regarded as standing for Luxus rather than Leicht! You can also recognise from this point on that the SL models were roadsters or available with removable hard tops, while the SLC models were the fixed roof coupes. Underneath they would be the same cars but the SL versions were for the real sports car enthusiast.

While the 230SL was not quite as fast as the 300SL in the straight line, the

Both the 'Gullwing' 300SL and the Roadster versions were fast, exotic and expensive. It occurred to Mercedes-Benz that the market was there for a sports car built in more numbers and to a less exotic specification, but keeping the overall look that had proved so successful. The result was the 190SL. Based on the chassis of the 180 sedan and powered by the four cylinder 105bhp engine, the car looked faster and more sporting than it actually was. But there is no denying the good looks.

Left: The 220 was a popular development of the 180 range. As with most Mercedes-Benz model ranges over the years, there was a cabriolet version. This is the 1960 220SE.

Right and below: After the raw power of the 300SL and the damp squib of the 190SL, Mercedes-Benz came up with a far better compromise between the two. The 230SL was actually a better handling car than the 300SL, with higher performance than the 190 SL. It was powered by the 2.3-liter version of the six cylinder engine producing 150bhp.

new car did not have the swing axle suspension that made the 300SL a handful to drive cross country at any great pace. The 230SL was a far better handling car. Initial claims talked of 170bhp although these were later reduced to say the 2306cc unit produced 150bhp at 5500rpm – still impressive by the standards of the day and thankfully a great improvement on the 190SL.

One other noticeable aspect of this car was that Continental and Firestone actually designed and produced a new range of tires specifically for the model. This is more common for performance cars today, but was a new development in the early 1960s.

When the six cylinder engine was enlarged to 2496cc and installed in the 250 sedans in 1965 it was logical that it should be fitted to the SL and SLC range. This happened in March 1967 and although the 2.5-liter did not actually have more power, the larger valves and redesigned cylinder head gave the unit ten percent more torque. This meant that both acceleration and top speed were improved but also that the car could be driven in a more relaxed manner. This did, in this writer's view, soften the car a shade.

But there was more to come in the form of the 2.8-liter in 1968 called, naturally enough, the 280SL and 280SLC. Power was up by 10bhp and the top speed was now 121mph but the sharpness of the product was also gone. The car was prone to roll, the suspension more of a compromise on the side of a comfortable ride rather than good handling. Whatever it is that makes a good sports car, the 280SL and its SLC sister were rather lacking.

But it didn't seem to matter any more. Mercedes-Benz had tapped into a market that demanded an easier, softer car, but still with fair performance. The 280SL remained in production until 1971, still visually similar to the original 230SL, but now a very different machine.

By the beginning of the 1970s the looks of the SL were decidedly dated. Some 50,000 models were produced, making a production success but time had come to change, and the change came with the V8-engined 350SL and 350SLC coupe.

These cars had little in common with the models they replaced. The 3.5-liter V8 engine with Bosch electronic fuel injection produced 200bhp and 211lb ft of torque. The styling matched the S-class sedans, smooth simple lines with large almost wrap-around rectangular front headlights. The car's handling was rather more in keeping with what people expected from a sports car. The semi-trailing rear end had to be treated with respect, especially in the wet, and it became rather necessary to ensure you were on the right tires as Mercedes-Benz had a policy to make the car available on a variety of different rubbers. At the time, some tire companies had rather better products than others and this became highlighted on a performance car like this one.

There was something of a problem with the model. When the V8 engine was fitted with all the necessary paraphernalia to meet the American emission requirements, the US-spec cars were hopeless performers. It is somewhat ironic, therefore, when you consider that the smog reducing requirements were designed in part to force manufacturers to consider smaller more efficient units, while in the case of the Mercedes-Benz sports car, they resulted in the German company putting an even bigger, more powerful engine under the hood to ensure that it still had some performance when it landed across the Atlantic. And so the 4.5-liter V8 was introduced to the range making the 450SL and 450SLC.

These models also had new rear suspension which much improved the handling. The 225bhp available further improved the performance, and they were also very well appointed. In short, the 450SL may not have looked much different to the original 350SL but it was a far better car.

Quite whether a sports car with an integrally designed removeable hard top should actually be called a coupe is difficult to answer. As the pictures on these pages indicate, the Mercedes-Benz sports car range has developed over the years and each of these models is fitted with a hard top. Whether the owners ever bothered to take them off is also questionable. *Above and right* the 280SL. *Above right* the 350SL.

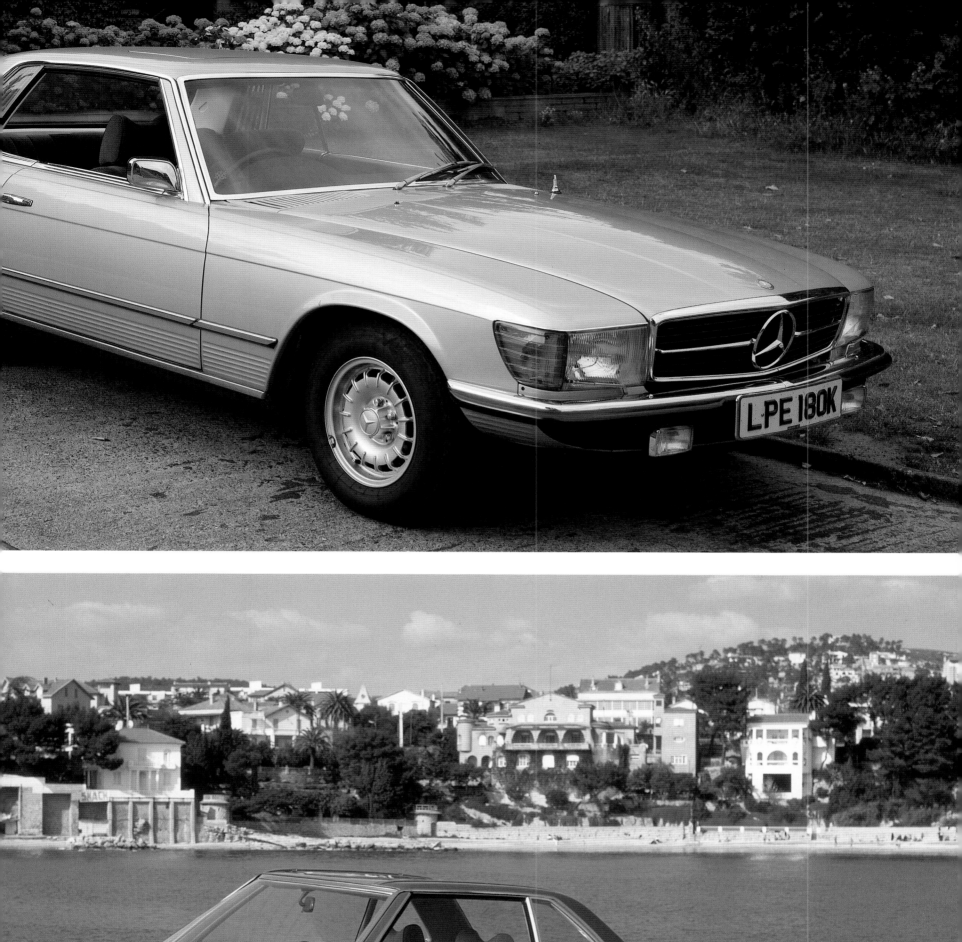

Right: The handling characteristics of the 450 SLs of the late 1970s were excellent. The chassis proving good enough to take the V8 engine when the car was sent to America.

Below: The Mercedes-Benz sports cars had all the luxury appointments of the sedan versions.

Far right: The smaller capacity V8-engined sports car, the 380 SLC was aimed directly at sales in America and the Middle East.

So good were its general chassis characteristics that it was the model that was first to get the brand new 5-liter V8 engine that was destined for the new S-class range of sedans. The new all-aluminum engine gave 240bhp at 5000rpm and a thumping 298lb ft of torque at only 3200rpm. This made the 1978 450SL 5.0 and 450SLC 5.0 impressive performers with a claimed top speed of 140mph (originally, they were not called 500SL or 500SLC because Mercedes-Benz wanted to keep the 500 designation for the as yet un-announced sedan car range). There was also wood veneer in the cockpit stressing that this was more of a gentleman's sporting coupe rather than an arm-twirling hairy-chested sports machine. Despite which, Hannu Mikkola's rallying exploits in the 450 SLC 5.0 did much to cement an encouraging sporting image.

Although the introduction of the exciting new V8 engine was an important point in the history of the company, it also signalled the end of an era for these sports versions. When the alloy engine was introduced in 1979, along with the smaller 3.8-liter version for the old 350, the new S-class sedans could really out-shine the sports department. Better aerodynamically, lighter and better handling they could out-perform the SLC. The result was the announcement in 1981 of the 380 and 500SEC, coupe versions of the new S-class sedans aimed directly at sales in America and the Middle East.

The SL range, of course, remained on what was now a rather dated chassis design. Nevertheless, an open-topped car will always have appeal. In the case of the SL, however, you did need to be rather athletic as the fold down soft top was extremely cumbersome and heavy – a fault throughout the history of these models. But the market remained and so did the model. In 1986, it was revised. Bigger inlet valves, revised camshaft timing and better breathing increased power to 265bhp in the case of the 500 and 218bhp for the 380 version. It was at this time, however, that the smallest engine version, the 280SL, was dropped altogether, replaced by a version using the 3-liter six cylinder engine that had been introduced into the sedan range in 1984. The engine size did mean that the car could be designated 300SL – not really a patch on the original 300SL, of course. All SL models were fitted with ABS (Anti-Blockierung which we know as Anti-Lock Braking System).

Visually the updated range had a new front spoiler, larger diameter wheels and lower profile tires, with the 500SL getting a small lip spoiler on the trunk lid – the latter always looking a little tacky on what was still a class automobile. Its aerodynamic qualities could be questioned, but it was far more a simple way of noting that this was the top of the range 5-liter SL.

But these revisions were but a stop gap. If the lack of real change gives the impression that the company had forgotten its sports car heritage and was prepared to let it fade away, then we must erase that immediately. The SL range in the late 1980s was based on the oldest chassis arrangement still available at Mercedes-Benz. In the design department there was a new model taking shape, a new sports car, a car that Mercedes-Benz has called 'a new beginning'.

The new sports car unveiled in 1989, is the fourth generation of SL and it is light years ahead of that first model. From any angle, it is a truly stunning design. It is longer, wider and slightly heavier than the model it replaced but to be fair the only thing it has in common with the previous car is the SL designation. The shape is clean, crisp, undeniably glamorous and undeniably Mercedes-Benz. The design now incorporates integrated bumper bars which meet all US regulations. Safety and aesthetic design are also matched perfectly with the use of a retractable roll-over bar. The design team wanted the clean, completely open effect of a true roadster but also needed to meet any criticism with regard to safety. The latest SL, therefore, has a roll bar which lies flush to the body line completely out of sight but is raised automatically in just 0.3 seconds should the car's massive sensor system react to frontal impact, side impact, rear impact or a potential roll. The system is so effective that the car passed all US standards usually applied to completely closed cars. The aim was to design and build the safest open topped car in the world and they have spent four and a half years and $15 million doing just that.

The car's suspension system is equally impressive. It includes the Adaptive Damping System (ADS) which electronically adapts and alters the car's suspension characteristics to suit the road surface. There are five sets of sensors throughout the car monitoring vertical movement of the wheels; road speed, angle of the steering wheel and load. The electronic messages, some 100 per second, are sent to a control unit which monitors them and decides which of the four optimum damper settings are best for the situation. This all happens remarkably quickly with adjustment taking only 0.1 second. To get that into perspective, if the car is doing 60mph and the front wheels hit a bump that sends that information to the control unit, the message will be relayed to the rear suspension, altering the setting as necessary before the rear wheels hit that same bump!

The suspension also automatically reacts to performance motoring,

Left: One of the impressive things about a Mercedes-Benz convertible is the neat way the soft top stows away at the rear. This makes the car at its most attractive with the top fully down.

Above: The 420 SEC has the smooth rounded look of the modern Mercedes-Benz.

Right and overleaf: If the 'Gullwing' Mercedes-Benz was the most desirable sports car of the 1950s, then the present day luxury sports car that sets new standards has to be the new SL range. As can be seen overleaf, it is available as a soft top or with fully trimmed hard top.

The 500SL is a model well worthy of concluding this chapter on Mercedes-Benz sports cars. It's not a furiously quick sports car, far more a rapid, well-appointed Grand Tourer built in the best traditions. And it stays that way whether you want the top up or down, it all happens at the touch of a button.

The multi-valve philosophy is carried over to the V8. The unit has been strengthened with the use of a micro-alloyed tempered steel crankshaft and con rods to cope with an impressive increase in power. The 32 valve unit will now deliver 326bhp at 5500rpm (compared to 265bhp on the old unit).

The 300SL has the option of either five speed manual or four speed automatic while the 500SL only has the automatic option. The performance of the car now means that the top speed of the 500SL is governed to 155mph. (Without the electronic governor it is likely that the car would top 170mph). There are other aspects of the car's design whereby its performance is 'controlled'. You cannot, for instance, do standing start acceleration runs screeching the tires and leaving great black lines on the road. The car has an anti-skid element where sensors pick up the first indication that the wheels are about to lose grip and instantly reduce power – even if you still have your foot hard down. The same thing happens if the car detects the rear wheels are about to slide in an over-enthusiastic cornering maneuver. This is not to say that it is a dull car, obviously the performance is terrific and it will remain one of the fastest accelerating automatics in the world – the bonus is that it has a 326bhp engine that can be driven by anyone. It's not a frighteningly powerful sports car but a rapid, luxurious, Grand Tourer. And the soft top, is it still heavy and awkward? Hardly. At a push of a button the top can be raised or lowered. It takes about 20 seconds and you don't even have to get out of the car.

The showroom price of these models matches the investment and the high level of performance and creature comforts included in the specification. As soon as they were announced, a considerable waiting list was established and that was before people even had the opportunity to drive the cars. For those lucky few who will own one of these beauties, the waiting – however long – will have been worthwhile and the drive, when it comes, will not disappoint.

The 500SL is a worthy vehicle to conclude this chapter on the Mercedes-Benz sports cars, but in truth, it doesn't actually end there. As this book is being written, the company is putting the final touches to a new V12 engine and this will find its way into the SL. A breath-taking prospect really, even with the top up.

lowering the car by 0.6in at speeds over 75mph to aid stability and reduce the aerodynamic drag.

All these new fangled tricks and the obvious high level of occupant comfort inevitably give the car a weight penalty, but these are completely negated by the developments to the power units. There are three versions, the 300SL with its six cylinder unit, the 300SL-24 a multi-valve six cylinder and the 500SL with its 5-liter V8. The 'base' model uses the 3-liter six cylinder that is also in the present 300E and 300SE sedans. A slightly different specification including a change of camshaft gives a small increase of power and torque over the sedans, up to 190bhp and 192lb ft. The 300-24 engine is based on the same unit but with four valves per cylinder head. The advantages of multi-valve designs are that they rev higher and the 300-24 produces maximum power of 231bhp at 6300rpm.

Motorsporting Glory
– Past and Present

The story of Mercedes-Benz motorsporting activities over the last 90 years – yes, it has been that long – is one of waves of involvement. The waves do not indicate a fickle company that cannot make up its corporate mind, but one of a company that competes when it feels it necessary. It has been forced to cease on two occasions when the program has been interrupted by global conflict and it has also withdrawn at times when its total domination has made any continuation a pointless waste of resources.

As this is being written, the great Mercedes motorsporting might is again dominating, this time in world sports prototype car racing. Will the company again say enough and walk away victors or will they, as is rumored, take the plunge and enter the Grand Prix Formula One Championship?

That is for future authors to recall. Here we will concentrate on the facts. And the facts go back as far as the cars themselves.

The Pre-1914 Period

Back at the turn of this century, motorsport was in its infancy – and was certainly a far cry from what we know today. There were no racing circuits with beautifully smooth tarmac surfaces, covered grandstands and television cameras. Motorsport occurred on normal roads; great marathon races were held from city to city. The roads were not as we would recognise them today either, mere dirt tracks, liberally covered with rocks and boulders – the kinds of roads that present day rally cars would consider rough!

For the cars in the early 1900s, the roads were just one of a number of hazards. The cars were ill-handling and difficult to drive quickly. Poor quality tires added to the rough roads and led to both punctures and accidents. Safety was not high on the list of necessities for a race car at the start of the century; there were no helmets or seat belts for the drivers. With long races, each team ran with a driver and mechanic, the latter there to mend both the mechanicals and change the wheels because of the numerous punctures. It was tough for both man and machine.

As we have already said, Karl Benz personally disapproved of racing. It is not perhaps surprising, therefore, that his early race cars were known for their reliability, not speed. The first recorded Benz racer was in the Paris – Rouen Trials in 1894 driven by the French importer Emile Roger.

Benz did, however, recognise the commercial importance of the sport and by 1908 the factory was heavily committed. Hemery drove one of the 120bhp racers on the St Petersburg – Moscow race, a 438 mile battle over appalling roads. The Benz won with a staggering average speed of over 50mph. Races both in Europe and America continued.

The most noteworthy Benz was the monstrous Blitzen (Lightning) of 1909. This chain driven device had a 21,504cc engine, despite being only four cylinders. It was claimed to develop 200bhp and on one flying mile competition at Daytona Beach was said to have reached just over 140mph. This magnificent beast held the World Land Speed Record from 1909 to 1924.

It is true to say, however, that Gottlieb Daimler's Mercedes racing cars overshadowed Benz. During this period, the most coveted prize in motorsport was the Gordon Bennett Cup and this was won by a 90bhp Mercedes in 1903, a great triumph as a big fire at the factory meant that it was the only Mercedes in the race. Despite many successes, Daimler actually withdrew from racing in 1908 because of the increasing costs. Privately entered Mercedes did still compete and gained some successes to keep the name to the fore.

The official return came in 1913, with the major pre-war triumph a year later at the 1914 French Grand Prix. The political tension in Europe at the time was high, making this event far more than just another race; national pride and prestige was at stake. Mercedes took the event seriously enough to have practised at the circuit outside Lyons for months before. Five of the four cylinder 115bhp Daimler cars were entered and the team dominated the whole race with a one-two-three finish. It was a staggering blow to the French in particular who believe their machines to be supreme. Months later and the whole of Europe was at war.

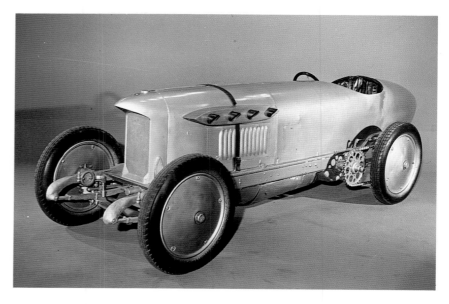

Previous page: How appropriate; Mercedes-Benz, numbers one, two and three, across the front row of the grid. The date is 1927 and the place is the famous Nurburgring. The cars are the supercharged S models with their 6.8-liter, 180bhp engines. The winner? Why Rudolf Caracciola in car number one, of course.

Above and above right: The Blitzen Benz was a legend in its own race time. It won many events and actually held the land speed record at over 140mph for many years and this at the turn of the century. The engine appeared in various forms up to an extraordinary capacity of 21.5 liters.

Left: The 1914 Grand Prix Mercedes. This model dominated motor racing at the time.

Right: The Benz racer on the 1903 Paris-Madrid, the distortion on the picture helping make the driver and riding mechanic look like beings from another planet.

Above: The 1914 Grand Prix Mercedes race cars were dominant — hence the smiles on the faces of driver Louis Wagner and his riding mechanic.

Left: Thankfully these cars are not reserved for museum only viewing. They do occasionally come out to compete. This is a 1914 GP Mercedes at the British hillclimb venue of Prescott — some 61 years after the car was built.

Right: This is the 'teardrop' Benz that caused such a stir when it appeared at Monza in 1923. With its mid-mounted engine behind the driver it was well ahead of its time. It did little on race tracks but had some success as a hillclimb vehicle.

The Silver Years

Understandably, recovery after the First World War restricted the Mercedes race program. The first post-war recorded model was the 28/95 entered for the 1921 Targa Florio where it finished second. A year later came the supercharged version based on the sports cars of the time, and this program was increased after the amalgamation of the two companies in 1926, giving the company reasonable success up until the early 1930s. Much of this was due to the caliber of drivers like the young German Rudolf Caracciola who was successful in both races and hillclimbs. It is worth remembering that many European hillclimbs were as important for a company's prestige as full-blown races and the supercharged Mercedes sports car achieved many such successes. But things became even more impressive with the announcement of the new Grand Prix formula for 1934.

Motorsport's governing body had become increasingly worried about the development of the cars, most of which had far more power than they could safely handle. To ensure that a new type of racing car was built for GPs, a weight limit of 750kgs was set.

Again national prestige was at stake and Mercedes-Benz received a grant of $80,000 from the German government to build a new racing car. Despite what was at the time a large amount of money, Hans Nibel and his design team spent this, and a considerable extra amount in a mere 10 months building the new W25.

The prototype was shown to Hitler in January 1934. It had a lightweight, extensively drilled chassis with independent wishbone suspension at the front and a swinging rear axle. The W25 had a hydraulic braking system (most cars were still using mechanical systems). The first model had a straight eight 3360cc supercharged engine developing 314bhp.

Although the W25 was a big car, Nibel had used a lot of light alloy castings in the construction, expensive at the time but considered essential to be able to get the car down to the new weight limit. When the cars were weighed for their first race at the Nurburgring for the Eifel GP, team manager Alfred Neubauer found that the white Mercedes-Benz racers were exactly 1kg over the limit. But how could this be? They had spent all this money building a new

car, with all the latest technology, yet it was 1kg over the weight limit. The story goes that Neubauer had the cars stripped of their white paint down to the bare alloy and when they were weighed in the morning, they were down to the 750kg limit. It was this that got the cars their now famous nickname The Silver Arrows.

(If that seems a little unlikely, it must be remembered that the cars were made of hand-beaten aluminum and therefore would have been very uneven. Before they were painted, a lot of filler was used to make the surface smooth. It was the removal of the filler, as much as the paint, that got the car down to the weight limit).

The first Silver Arrow won at Eifel in 1934 and it was the start of one of the most stunning eras of motor racing – certainly the great epoch in German racing history. In that first year, the new W25 won four of the major international events. To put the pure performance of the cars in perspective, in that first year, Caracciola was timed at just over 180mph – but there was more to come.

In 1935, the W25B was a development chassis, now with a 3990cc engine producing 430bhp, and it won nine of the ten major international events; Caracciola taking five wins himself.

It must be mentioned here that Mercedes cars did not quite have it their own way all the time. Ferdinand Porsche (who later went on to produce the now famous sports cars) had worked for Mercedes at the design stage of the W25. Originally, Porsche had suggested a rear-engined design for the car but this was not agreed by Nibel. Porsche left to progress his design. This was taken up by the four manufacturer combine of Audi, DKW, Wanderer and Horsch, and the project was called the Auto Union. It was these rear-engined Porsche-designed cars, which, like Mercedes, were running with government subsidy, that were the major competition. If 1935 was undoubtedly Mercedes' year, for 1936 the tables were turned and it was a triumph for Auto Union.

For 1937 a new 3-liter Grand Prix formula for supercharged cars was proposed although it was decided at the last minute to allow the previous years' cars to continue for a final year. This led to the W125 which had a 5.6-liter straight eight providing a massive 600bhp. The major problem was to get all this power down to the ground – the W25 has been said to have been capable of wheel-spinning at 150mph in top gear! To overcome this problem, much work was done on the chassis.

The driving team was still led by Caracciola, now at his peak, but for this year a young Englishman, Richard Seaman, joined the team. Caracciola took a streamlined version of the car to a new class world record of 268.9mph. The record was set on the Frankfurt – Darmstadt autobahn, this particular piece of German freeway being regularly used for record-breaking, closed for the occasion, of course.

Above: Rudolf Caracciola enjoying the spoils of victory having won the 1926 German GP for Mercedes-Benz.

Left: A further development of the 'teardrop' principle for this 1924 Benz.

Right: One of the all-time great racers. The W125 was capable of 200mph on some circuits. One of the drivers who made his name in the car was the Englishman Richard Seaman. This was the era of the Silver Arrows.

The new 3-liter formula was in full force for 1938 and Mercedes responded with the W154. The idea of the new formula was to make the cars heavier and less powerful, therefore cutting down the speed, as once again the authorities were concerned about safety. The Mercedes-Benz team, however, was now the undoubted master of the track and the new chassis development made a car that, although less powerful, actually handled better and had better brakes. It was nearly as fast as the previous W125. Richard Seaman won the German Grand Prix that year – much to the displeasure of Adolf Hitler – with the Mercedes team dominating the entire season.

The following year saw the W163 Mercedes, with its wonderfully sleek body and 430bhp. Success was still theirs, but not without cost. In 1939 Dick Seaman crashed at Spa and died of his injuries.

By now the rest of Europe was wondering what it could do to beat the Silver Arrows. For the prestigious Tripoli Grand Prix the Italians thought they had the answer by changing the rules (this was a non-Championship race so they could do this) and allowing only 1.5-liter supercharged cars. This was to give Alfa Romeo (led by a certain Enzo Ferrari) and Maserati the best chance of victory. To everyone's great surprise, Mercedes turned up with the W165, a scaled down version of the W163, powered by a 1.5-liter V8. It had been designed and built in just eight months and Caracciola and Herman Lang duly dominated the race thoroughly to humiliate the Italians.

It may have only been five years, but 1934 – 1939 was a supreme time for Grand Prix racing. The battles between the Mercedes and the Auto Unions (which also ran in bare aluminum and were also given the title Silver Arrows) were the stuff of legends. Some color film does exist of this period, notably of the British Grand Prix at Donington. To watch it today is to sit in awe of the cars and the drivers. Capable of 200mph, in straight line top speed they would almost be a match for Formula One cars today. But to see how the drivers had to wrestle the cars around the corners, however, shows otherwise. These guys were very special.

Again the racing program was curtailed by war. It was to be 15 years before Mercedes would return to the victory rostrum.

Above and left: The 1938 W154 was powered by a 3-liter V12 engine producing 450bhp. The car is seen in the hands of classic car racing expert Neil Corner. Although this is a modern picture, the Auto Union in the background makes it quite a special 'period piece'.

Above right: The 1935 GP season began at Monaco and it began well for Mercedes-Benz when the Italian Luigi Fagioli won in the W125. He is shown here ahead of the Maserati of Sofetti.

Right: The W163 was a more streamlined development of the W154. The supercharged V12 engine would produce over 480bhp. Not surprisingly the car won five of the seven GPs in 1939.

Triumph And Tragedy

Once again then, global conflict had curtailed the Mercedes-Benz motorsport program. That is not meant as a trite statement, far more that when understanding the massive effect both wars had on the German economy, one could believe that motorsport would take a long time to return to any manufacturers' future plans.

Rumors of the Mercedes-Benz return to the track had been circulating for a long while before it actually happened in 1952 with the 300SL. This was a 3-liter Sport Leicht (light) a closed coupe sports car with the now universally recognised gullwing doors. These doors were not a gimmick but necessary due to the design of the car's chassis. Light, but with only a very modest 175bhp from the six cylinder engine these unique sports cars were not expected to be particularly successful.

However, the writing was on the wall at the debut event, the highly prestigious Mille Miglia sports car race in Italy when Karl Kling and Hans Klenk finished second to Ferrari. In 1952, the 300SL won the next four sports car races that it entered including the pearl of all sports car endurance challenges, the Le Mans 24 Hours. It's fair to say that Kling and Klenk (a fabulously emotive sounding driving pairing) were fortuitous to win Le Mans that year, as victory came through faster cars' failures, but, as the motorsport maximum goes, 'To finish first, first you have to finish.' Mercedes-Benz reliability was never in doubt.

The company promptly withdrew the following year, not from some rush of blood to the corporate head, but to plan the real challenge – a return to Formula One. A new 2.5-liter formula had been decided, effective from 1954 and Mercedes-Benz intended to be there. But this was now a completely new game. Lessons from pre-war GP cars and the successful 300SL were of little use to the German team. A carbon copy of the Italian Ferrari or Maserati race cars would seem to have been a logical development, but not to Mercedes-Benz. A clean sheet of paper was pulled over the drawing board; from it came a new engine and the gorgeous W196.

The engine itself was something of a buck against the tradition for the day. V8s and V12s were the rage, certainly from the Italians (a fact that has continued to this very day), but the Mercedes-Benz team looked towards functionality and purpose. The result was a straight eight because it had far less auxiliary drives than the V designs, and if angled to one side, could allow a very low hood line. If a straight eight sounds considerably less technically adventurous than a V12, then just wait and listen. The new Mercedes-Benz engine had desmodromic arrangement of camshaft and rockers which allowed optimum filling of the combustion chambers and did away with return valve springs which both saved space and allowed for greater valve lift. With the latter a missed gear by the driver would not lead to the over-revved engine dropping a valve and meeting a piston on the way up! They were not completely bullet-proof, of course, but they were a significant design advance of the day.

The lower center of gravity from the angled position of the front engine was also a design plus. The small-diameter spaceframe chassis allowed for a low sleek all-enveloping bodywork design and it is this, more than the then unknown technical tweaks, that caused the greatest stir when the car was launched in 1954. The other great development was team manager Neubauer's selection of Juan Manuel Fangio as the number one driver.

Fangio and Kling took a debut one-two victory for the 1954 French GP after the Ferraris of Mike Hawthorn and Froilan Gonzalez had retired. Yet for the British GP, mere weeks later, the German team was beaten. This was not, however, indicative of being uncompetitive but more the controversial all-enveloping bodywork which made vision from the cockpit more difficult for the drivers – Fangio confirmed this by hitting a number of the barrels used to mark out the circuit. For the German GP at the Nurburgring an open wheel body was debuted – and Fangio duly won.

He followed that in the Swiss GP. Then the Italian, where the German team became much impressed by a young British driver called Stirling Moss who kept his Maserati ahead of the Mercedes for 45 laps only for it to fail close to the finish.

That first season did not show the W196 to be invincible, although it was fast and it was reliable. Mercedes-Benz did clinch the manufacturers' title, largely due to the fabulous driving talent of Fangio who deservedly took his second drivers' title.

One season's experience was all that was necessary, however. For the following year, Stirling Moss joined the team to drive the lighter, more powerful 300SLRs. Despite their title, they were a development of the Grand Prix cars rather than of the 1952 300SL sports car. They were also designated the W196S. The car was, therefore, able to compete in both GP racing and the sports car series – high on Mercedes-Benz prestige priorities.

The W196 was built to meet the new 2.5-liter racing formula. It originally appeared with all-enveloping, streamlined bodywork (*right*). However, the car was most successful with open wheels (*above left*).

Top: It has to be Monaco and the driving style of the number six Mercedes-Benz W196 just has to be that of Stirling Moss. He is seen trying to go round the outside of team-mate Juan Fangio in the similar car. Fabulous photograph.

In true Mercedes-Benz tradition there was yet another unique development. Many companies were looking at disc brake designs while Mercedes-Benz wished to stick to drums but added an outrageous air brake whereby part of the rear bodywork could be raised for particularly demanding situations – like at the end of the Mulsanne Straight at Le Mans where the 300SLR could reach 180mph.

The 300SLR was a success. Period. Victory for Fangio in his home GP in Argentina was followed by Moss winning the Mille Miglia no less than 30 minutes ahead of his South American team-mate. Fangio and Moss were one-two at the Monaco GP until a freak double technical failure side-lined both cars. It was a mere hiccup. Fangio-Moss were one-two in the Eifelrennen at the Nurburgring, one-two in the Belgian GP.

Motorsport, however, was devastated by a freak accident at that year's Le Mans 24 Hours. Pierre Levegh, driving a 300SLR, came up behind a slower car, cannoned off it and was catapulted into the packed grandstands. Over 80 spectators were killed. The Mercedes-Benz team withdrew – with Moss and Fangio holding a two lap lead over the Jaguars at the time. It was a monumental disaster. Switzerland has never held a motor race since that date. The 1955 French and German GPs were cancelled.

Mercedes-Benz underlined their supremacy in such a sad year with three consecutive one-two victories in the last three races of the season; Fangio in Holland, Moss in Britain and Fangio in Italy.

In sports car racing, the company's domination was just as comprehensive; one-two for Fangio and Moss in Sweden, one-two-three for the Dundrod Tourist Trophy. Having won the drivers' and manufacturers' titles already, Neubauer sent two cars to the Targa Florio to take the sports car championship from Ferrari. Moss, with co-driver Peter Collins, had an accident and went off the road for nine minutes, yet returned and won by nearly five minutes, with Fangio and Kling second.

At the end of 1955, there was nothing left to prove. And that, with the terrible publicity associated with the Le Mans disaster, saw Mercedes-Benz withdraw from racing.

The Rough Stuff

It would be wrong to think that Mercedes-Benz completely ignored motorsport after 1955. Although initially it was not as committed as the racing team, the factory did tackle rallying with Walter Schock and Rolf Moll winning the 1956 European Championship in a 300SL.

The second half of the 1950s saw a few scattered triumphs with 300SLs, but things grew more important when a full works supported effort began in 1960 with Schock and Moll winning the Monte Carlo Rally, with 220SE sedans also coming second and third. This great pairing won many other rallies for Mercedes-Benz; the Acropolis, Safari and the Argentinian Gran Premio which was more a road race than a rally.

67759

The long distance events became the domain of Mercedes-Benz especially when driven by the balding, middle-aged Stuttgart hotelier Eugen Bohringer.

At the end of the 1960s, works support was withdrawn until the heavily media-promoted London-Sydney Rally of 1977. Mercedes-Benz entered what was really a British importer's team with German assistance but the record books still say it was a Mercedes-Benz one-two for the British teams Andrew Cowan/Colin Malkin/Mike Broad and Tony Fowkes/Michael O'Gorman.

Marathon experts Cowan and Malkin then won the 1978 South American Rally in a 450SLC and the 1979 Safari Rally was all but won by Hannu Mikkola in a 450SLC 5.0 who dominated the event until a freak accident with a low-flying bird forced him back to second place.

Although not comprehensive, or particularly heavily supported by the factory, the rallying successes of the 1960s and 1970s did keep the Mercedes-Benz marque in the public eye concentrating once again on reliability of its sports cars.

Left: The view from behind the wheel of the 1955 Mille Miglia 300 SLR. The drivers legs go either side of the transmission tunnel.

Bottom left: The 1955 Le Mans 24 hour race saw the 300 SLRs. Unable to match the braking power of the Jaguars – the British team introduced disc brakes at this race – the German team introduced this unique air brake system. This race will be remembered, however, by the accident that occurred to Mercedes-Benz driver Pierre Levegh who crashed into the grandstand. Mercedes-Benz withdrew not only from that event, but racing as a whole.

Mercedes-Benz has had a small but significant influence on World class rallying. When the events were based closely on road cars and reliability was the key, the German factory proved its worth. *Above:* A Type 219 on the East African safari in 1960. *Bottom right:* The same event, this time in 1979 with the 450 SLC 5.0. *Center:* Probably Mercedes-Benz's best rallying result – victory in the 1977 London – Sydney marathon.

Return Of The Silver Arrows

They came, they saw, they conquered and they withdrew. The Mercedes-Benz motorsport history and the magnificent periods of domination in the 1930s and 1950s does have a certain pattern to it. So when the factory officially announced its return on 12 January 1988 one could be forgiven for thinking foregone conclusion, third time, same thing.

That would be a little unkind and also an insult to the quality of the teams that the new Mercedes-Benz Silver Arrows have been beating in the last few years. When the company returned to the track there was Porsche, totally dominant in sports car racing throughout the 1970s and there was Jaguar returning to the world scene after nearly as long an absence as Mercedes-Benz themselves. And there was Japan, having been spoon-fed the glory of the early years, both Nissan and Toyota want their share of the cake now. Sports car racing, especially the Le Mans 24 Hours holds a special significance to the Japanese, they want to win it badly.

And, of course, the whole sports prototype championship had changed. Run under Group C rules it was necessary for any new car to have power and reliability as before but it was also a matter of adhering to a fuel consumption formula, the antipathy of motorsport, perhaps, but economy was now the god of this class of racing.

Mercedes-Benz made the sensible first move in using a small, relatively successful privateer as the factory's doorway back to the track. Peter Sauber must have thought all his Christmasses had come at once when Mercedes-Benz took an interest in his small Swiss-based racing team. Sauber had introduced himself in 1984 when racing his cars with BMW engines, the Swiss engineer having written to Mercedes-Benz to ask if he could use the wind tunnel at Unterturkheim and the company agreeing. His chassis were good, his preparation excellent and he impressed Mercedes-Benz when he arrived

at the wind tunnel, so much so that when he asked about the possibility of using the 5-liter Mercedes-Benz engine in his next chassis, they started to listen. Sauber was convinced that the V8 had all the right qualities for the new fuel consumption formula.

The first Sauber-Mercedes, the C8, was actually destroyed in a practice accident at its debut at Le Mans in 1985. Mercedes-Benz engineers, notably Hermann Hiereth, head of the engine research division of the Swiss team and when extra sponsorship was available from Yves St Laurent, a short season was planned for 1986. Sauber duly delivered, proved the competitiveness of the combination and won at the Nurburgring.

Understandably, people now asked the question whether this team represented Mercedes-Benz return to racing. Initially the factory continued to say no, it was just a private team given factory engines. In January 1988, however, the board agreed to announce, formally, that this was a joint project. These 1988 Sauber-Mercedes were actually dark blue but proved very competitive. That year, arch rivals Jaguar won the World title.

In 1989, the dark blue paint came off, but not of course to reveal aluminum. This time, to get the right effect on the glassfiber bodywork, the cars were actually painted silver. The Silver Arrows were back.

The Sauber C9 chassis design was good, not necessarily the best in the field but coupled with the 5.0-liter V8 turbocharged Mercedes-Benz engines, the result was emphatic. The power, reliability and that all-important fuel consumption were the best of the field. The 1989 Sports Prototype World Championship went to Mercedes-Benz and to add to the domination, Jean-Louis Schlesser, Jochen Mass and Mario Baldi took first, second and third respectively in the drivers' championship – all driving Silver Arrows.

The icing on the cake also had to be the one-two finish in the Le Mans 24 Hours, handsomely beating Porsche and Jaguar. It certainly looked like history repeating itself. It also looked easy.

Above left: Mercedes-Benz return to racing was with the Sauber racing team. While the chassis was built by the Sauber team, the engine was a development of the production V8.

Above: Racing, even at club motor sport level, remains an important method of promoting the marque. This is a 190 in action during a British club meeting.

Right: The Silver Arrows return! Team shot of the Mercedes-Benz Group C sports prototype racer. The drivers behind the car emphasise just how low the car is.

For 1990, as this is written, it has looked even easier. The main competition from Jaguar was relatively poor, the British team having a terrible year. Mercedes-Benz took the 1990 title, with the only gap in the trophy cupboard being Le Mans – not because the Silver Arrows were beaten but because the German team did not enter after a particularly petty series of rows between the organisers and the motorsport governing body had led many to think the event would not take place at all. Mercedes-Benz had proven it was back at the forefront of world sports car racing.

But that is not the only branch of the sport where the three-pointed star is once again to the front. The German Touring Car Championship is a massively successful championship for standard sedan cars. Modifications are permitted but within strict guidelines, the cars that race are really the same cars that are for sale in the showrooms. It is for this reason that Mercedes-Benz introduced the 190E 2.6-16 Evolution II model in 1990. With its huge rear wing and enormous wheel and tire combination, the car looks a born racer while stationary in a parking lot. Once in the hands of the race teams, it is more than a match for the likes of BMW and Audi. The German Touring Car Championship is hugely popular throughout Europe thanks to satellite television. As always, motorsport improves the breed and helps sell the cars.

So with success with sedans and success with sports car racing, you can tell what is coming next can't you? A Mercedes-Benz decision to withdraw, all-conquering, for 1991. As this is being written that has not occurred. The World sports car championship should be far more competitive in 1991 with the new Peugeot Group C car and increasing Japanese interest, together with a promised improvement in Jaguar's competitiveness. There are also rumors, and public pressure to see Mercedes-Benz return to Grand Prix racing with a Formula One car.

If they do, you can guarantee one thing; they'll be silver.

Above: The road-going version of the 190 2.5-16 Evolution II was used as the base for the racing version that has done so well in the German Touring Car Championship.

The Sports Prototype World Championship went to the Mercedes-Benz team in 1989 (*left*) and 1990 (*right*). The Silver Arrows had returned to racing and to the winner's podium.

Researching The Future

There is one inescapable fact about being a successful mass production manufacturer; it don't come easy. The ability to make a quality range of motor cars is not something that appears overnight. The car that you and I drive today is what it is because of the amount of research and development that has gone into its design and production.

Just as at the beginning of this book we talked about Gottlieb Daimler and Karl Benz as pioneers in the field of automotive engineering, it is worth keeping in perspective the fact that, in principle, nothing has changed. In the very beginning we can focus on individual men of vision and ingenuity, but as the knowledge grows, and becomes more widely available, so the individual takes a back seat. Today we talk of advances not by the individual's name but by the company that devised them. Any successful company today must invest heavily in its Research and Development department to keep ahead. New car designs that are on the drawing boards of the major manufacturers today, will not make it into production for a number of years. You cannot change a model range or introduce a new development overnight. To stay ahead, therefore, you must work at it.

Mercedes-Benz has been well aware of the importance of the Research and Development department. You could well say that the philosophies of both Daimler and Benz exist today and have been evident in the company's direction throughout its history.

With Mercedes-Benz there is an undeniable second factor in that, as a German company, there have been moments when a desire for very positive national propaganda necessitated research projects. This, of course, was at its most prevalent before the outbreak of the Second World War, and it pushed the company in the direction of record breaking.

The highly successful Mercedes-Benz Grand Prix cars of the time were possessed of streamlined bodyshapes and this meant that they could be modified to challenge a number of class world speed records (5 to 8-liter). By the late 1930s they had pushed this International B class up to 269mph

(433kph). Impressive as this was, the major prize, of course, was the outright World Land Speed record. Around this time, Malcolm Campbell's Bluebird had taken the record over 300mph, followed by George Eyston's Thunderbolt that pushed the record to 345mph (555kph) in 1938. John Cobb snatched it back for Britain in the Railton, being the first man to reach 350mph only to see George Eyston crack 357mph the very next day! Cobb took the record back in 1939 with his 367mph run. The battle was fierce and the prestige of holding the record was enormous.

To this end, Mercedes-Benz set about building their own machine, the T80. Designed by Dr Porsche, it was to run with a massive aero engine from the Daimler-Benz aircraft subsidiary. This engine was a 44.5-liter V12 which in its more usual format would produce about 1700bhp. Mercedes-Benz engineers were convinced, however, that for the short duration of a Land Speed Record run, power could be turned up to nearer 3000bhp.

The T80 had a highly aerodynamic body with small "wing" outriders to increase stability at high speed. Underneath the body was a tubular space-frame chassis, a mid-mounted engine and six wheels; a pair at the front, and two sets in tandem to take the drive from the engine.

It was planned for the car to be driven by Hans Stuck, a driver who had a great reputation at the time for his record-breaking abilities, although he was something of a surprise choice since he also drove for Auto Union. The T80 was expected to top 400mph (640kph) and most experts believe it was well capable of just that. Unfortunately the outbreak of war signalled the end of the project.

The Wankel Years

Research and development costs a great deal and the benefits on the production line may not be seen for a number of years. It is little surprise, therefore, that the R&D department suffered the most during the reconstruction

Previous page: A special exhibition called Auto 2000 saw Mercedes-Benz build this gas turbine powered car of the future.

Left: Let the sunshine in. This is a solar powered Mercedes-Benz which took victory in the 1985 Tour de Sol. At one stage, driver Peter Bauer was averaging nearly 40mph.

Above and right: Mercedes-Benz has done a great deal of research and development using variations of the C111 experimental sports cars. The top picture shows C111/2 with a four rotor Wankel engine capable of 187mph. The aerodynamic version on the right was built in 1979 and has a turbocharged V8 engine and a top speed of over 250mph.

after the Second World War. It was not, in fact, until the 1960s that the public actually saw what Mercedes-Benz was working on.

The new project car was based on a deal that the German company had done with NSU to manufacture the Wankel engine back in 1961. Mercedes-Benz was well advanced in the development of the Wankel engine, but had not introduced this very different power unit into a production vehicle. The problems that were associated with NSU Ro80's engine when it was launched, problems that ultimately destroyed the company, did cause Mercedes-Benz to rethink the uses of the Wankel engine. Instead of a production vehicle, the company utilised the unit in an experimental format, enter the C111 Coupe.

The C111 was designed using the principle of a mid-engined racing car. It was very attractive too and caused a great deal of interest when announced at the 1969 Frankfurt Motor Show. But the car was far more than just a publicity exercise, it was a serious experimental machine; aerodynamic, lightweight and with a three rotor Wankel engine producing 280bhp, it was an impressive performer.

Three years later and C111/2 was shown. This now had a 4.8-liter four rotor Wankel engine developing 350bhp. The C111/2's performance was even more impressive, achieving 60mph in 4.8 seconds with a top speed of over 180mph. It was not just the way that it went that impressed, but also the way that it stopped. It was on this vehicle that Mercedes-Benz first developed their version of the anti-lock braking system. Developed with Bosch, the ABS system was later used on the next S-class, as was the front suspension of the C111/2 – thus emphasising the importance of this research machine.

Naturally, Mercedes-Benz was accumulating a great deal of information about the rotary engine, so why has this never been seen in a production car? It is thought that the company was never really able to overcome the engine's thirst for fuel and the emission levels that it ran at. With the 1973 fuel crisis, the engine was shelved, but that did not mean the end of the C111/2 project.

Now fitted with a turbocharged five cylinder diesel producing an impressive 190bhp, it set a number of international speed records previously held by Porsche and a gasoline-driven 911. At the Nardo circuit in southern Italy, the diesel C111 covered 10,000 miles at an average of 157mph (253kmph). The success of this record-breaking attempt led to the introduction of the 300SD turbo into the United States in 1974.

But the research department thought there was more to come from the project. The C111/3 was more streamlined having a longer wheelbase but smaller track (to cut down frontal area). The engine was again the diesel turbo, but, running higher boost pressure, now had 235bhp and a top speed just over 200mph.

The record breaking event was hampered by minor problems – like a hedgehog that crawled on to the track and damaged the car's front spoiler (the hedgehog too suffered serious damage) but Mercedes-Benz drivers still managed to break nine world records for a car in that class. To run at such high speed for such a long while demanded a fairly high ratio top gear, knowledge that was later used in production transmissions.

Looking Forward

Besides an enviable reputation for performance, Mercedes-Benz is also well-known for its stand on safety. And, like the performance machines we have just chronicled, much of the production pluses on today's models come from work done at the R&D department.

In 1972, Mercedes-Benz unveiled the Experimental Safety Vehicle. A 250 shell with modified 350SL running gear, the ESV was designed primarily to be a car that gave occupants safety from injury in a front or rear accident in speeds up to 50mph (80kph). It was this Mercedes-Benz that first had the energy absorbing bumpers that are familiar today. The car had automatic seat harness and air bags as well as a facility whereby the doors would not burst open in the event of an impact. All these items have since been incorporated into production models.

By the mid to late 1970s, the motor industry was looking hard at the big gas-guzzling car, particularly in America, Mercedes-Benz major export market. US Congress voted in CAFE (Corporate Average Fuel Economy) regulations and the heat was on the big-car manufacturer.

As you would expect if you have read all this book so far, Mercedes-Benz was not about to lay down and weep. The company had made its reputation from large roomy, expensive, vehicles and a worry over fossil fuel consumption was not about to change that. To meet the immediate CAFE demands, a smaller car was introduced (the 190), but also in 1980, Mercedes-Benz built a serious alternative, a gas turbine powered sedan.

The gas turbine is not thought a viable tool for small power units but for engines that need to produce around 150bhp it makes more sense. The gas turbine is more efficient in that it can use a variety of fuels and has very low

Above left and left: Mercedes-Benz has done much work on the safety aspects of automotive engineering. This 1972 vehicle was the test bed for the energy absorbing bumpers that are standard today. Thankfully the theory and practical use of these bumpers has been developed into a much more aesthetic version. The new 500SL (*left*) also has a roll over bar that is raised automatically should the car become inverted.

Right: It's not all smart sports cars – this is one of the Mercedes-Benz range of go-anywhere off-roaders. Built with Steyr Puch of Austria these four-wheel drive vehicles are available in a variety of models; from working commercial to luxury all-terrain machine.

Left: The present trend towards more economical vehicles has led Mercedes-Benz to producing more diesel engined models like this 350SD. While it is economical on fuel, nothing has been lost in the luxury interior.

Below left: The colored areas of this 300 series Mercedes-Benz are the area that can be recycled or are made from recycled material (see text).

Right: Getting stuck in with the Mercedes-Benz Gelandewagen.

emission levels. However, the drawbacks are that it is primarily a constant speed power unit – fine when the car is rushing along the autobahn but not much use in town traffic. Just how far down the line with this development the company is remains to be seen, but with increasing pressure on both the consumption and emission levels associated with the gasoline engine, you can guarantee that the gas turbine is still under consideration.

In the 1980s, safety is an even more significant subject for research, especially for a manufacturer that wants to sell cars in the United States. For Mercedes-Benz this means that they have a lot of crashes in Stuttgart; controlled crashes that is, in the form of impact tests. Not only does the company crash its own models, but also models from other manufacturers to see how they compare.

All cars have to pass a series of impact crash tests before they can be put on the market. Mercedes-Benz takes this many steps further at its special research center in Stuttgart where they are even able to produce a complete roll over situation, the most spectacular crash test of all.

But it would be wrong to get the idea that all this is done solely to make cars safer in an accident. Mercedes-Benz is very keen about what it calls 'active safety' – the preventive aspects that avoid accidents, making the car in such a way that is helps the driver to avoid the inevitable. This means better handling, better visibility and the ergonomically correct location of the controls.

A great deal of work is now going into active suspension developments. By this we mean a suspension system that works with an on-board computer so that sensors pick up changes in road surfaces and the car's attitude and compensate accordingly. Cornering without any discernable roll and a very flat, comfortable ride over extreme undulations are the potential benefits of this system. It could also be programmed to compensate for gusting side

winds to stop cars being blown off course. There is still a long way to go before this is readily available but Mercedes-Benz estimate that a fully active system for a mass production car is likely before the turn of the century.

Friendly Future

In our increasingly environmentally conscious society, the car is under more pressure than ever before. Motorised vehicles are not about to disappear as pressure from various political and social groups increases, but future legislation is likely to effect manufacturers more than ever in forthcoming years.

One of the major problems with the motor car is not the emissions that it produces but the fact that it is made from a huge variety of materials and when the car is finished, either through age or from an accident, all you are left with is a huge lump of junk. Sure there are scrap yards crushing old cars but they are far from efficient. Mercedes-Benz has, therefore, now introduced new research which could be a major environmental contribution.

The company has been recycling materials for a number of years – the glove compartment moldings have been made from recycled waste paper since the early 1950s, but the new S-class is the first major mass production car that has been designed and produced using a significant number of recyclable components and it is an important contribution to the problem, as we can see from this brief list.

PLASTIC: Some eight percent of the structure of today's cars is made from plastic which in the past has always been 'new' plastic, since it was thought impractical to recycle. Mercedes-Benz now recycle plastic plus waste from the production line and mix it with about 70 percent fresh polypropolene. It is hoped that the percentage of waste input could rise to 40-50 percent as the technique improves.

OIL: Engine oil is collected, refined, additives replaced and resold, and recommended by Mercedes-Benz. Brake fluid, particularly nasty stuff, is collected and sold to the chemical industry for use as a solvent.

BATTERIES: A car's battery has approximately 65 percent lead, 27.5 percent sulphuric acid and 7.5 percent plastic. Mercedes-Benz is now recycling all these substances which in the case of lead amounts to over 98,000 tons a year.

AIR CONDITIONING: The refrigerant for a car's air conditioning system has in the past been made from ozone-damaging CFCs. Mercedes-Benz has been replacing this from 1983 and developing the equipment to remove the fluid from a car's system without any escaping to the atmosphere. A hydro-flourocarbon is now used and will be in all Mercedes-Benz models from 1993.

BUMPERS: The insides of energy absorbing bumpers can be reused. The thermoplastic bumper itself can now be ground down and used to make secondary panels — like under the wheel arches, for instance, and hidden interior panels.

INSULATION: Waste textiles are used in the production of sound-deadening insulation. Mixed with resin this can also be used to make rigid panels for parcel shelves.

Most of the recycling is actually done at the source, the suppliers to Mercedes-Benz, but it is being orchestrated and encouraged by the company.

It would be wrong to turn the three-pointed star into a corporate halo, but the development of the environmental aspects of the new S-class is important. Mercedes-Benz has, of course, been under great pressure from the highly active German Green Party and the general pressure due to waste landfill problems that occur in West Germany. It's almost a case of if you can't dump it, use it. However, the developments are to be applauded and once again this only goes to stress the importance of a company's Research and Development department.

So from record-breaking to recycled paper for the glove compartment, those at Mercedes-Benz involved with research have a challenging and highly significant position within the company. You can be sure that both Gottlieb Daimler and Karl Benz would fully approve.

Superb vehicles like the latest 300 and 500 SL are only released on to the market after Mercedes-Benz research engineers have completed exhaustive test miles in all kinds of conditions.

Index

Figures in *italics* refer to illustrations

Acknowledgments

The author and publishers would like to thank the following people for their assistance in the production of this book:
David Eldred, who designed it, and Pat Coward, who compiled the index. The illustrations were supplied by the agencies and individuals listed below.

Bison Picture Library p31 lower
Neill Bruce pp 14 both, 66 top, 67, 68 both, 69 top, 74, 75 top, 76 lower, 77, 79 lower, 82 both, 83 lower, 92 both
Neill Bruce/The Peter Roberts Collection pp 6-7, 8 top, 10 top, 11 both, 12, 13 top, 15 bottom, 16 all three, 18-19, 20, 21 all three, 23 both, 24-25 top, 28 top, 30-31, 34 lower, 48, 49 top, 58-59, 60-61 both, 62 top, 64-65, 66 lower, 70, 72, 75 lower, 76 top, 84-85, 87 both, 88-89, 90-91, 93 both, 94, 95 both, 96 both, 106 top

Mercedes Benz pp 1, 2-3, 4-5, 8 bottom, 9 all three, 10 bottom, 13 bottom, 15 top, 22, 24, 25, 28 bottom, 29 both, 33 both, 34 top, 35 both, 36 top, 37 lower, 38, 40, 40-41 top, 41, 42, 43 both, 44 top, 46 both, 47 both, 49 lower, 50 both, 51, 52-53 all, 54 both, 55, 56 top, 62-63, 63 top, 69 lower, 71 top, 78, 79 top, 80-81, 83 top, 86 both, 89, 90, 97 all three, 98 (photo Colin Taylor), 99 top (Colin Taylor), 99 lower, 100-101 all three, 102-103, 104, 105 both, 106 lower, 108 both, 110 both
Andrew Morland pp 26-27, 30 bottom, 31 top, 32 both, 36 lower, 37 top, 39 both, 40-41 lower, 44 lower, 45 both, 56 lower two, 57, 71 lower, 73 all three, 107, 109

Neill Bruce would like to thank the Midland Motor Museum, Bridgnorth for assistance regarding the photographs on pp 66 top, 67, 68, 69 top.